Internships
in Psychology

Internships
in Psychology

The APAGS Workbook
for Writing Successful Applications
and Finding the Right Fit

Third Edition

Carol Williams-Nickelson,
Mitchell J. Prinstein,
and W. Gregory Keilin

American Psychological Association • Washington, DC

First Printing July 2012
Second Printing March 2013
Third Printing September 2016

Published by
American Psychological Association
750 First Street, NE
Washington, DC 20002
www.apa.org

To order
APA Order Department
P.O. Box 92984
Washington, DC 20090-2984
Tel: (800) 374-2721; Direct: (202) 336-5510
Fax: (202) 336-5502; TDD/TTY: (202) 336-6123
Online: www.apa.org/pubs/books
E-mail: order@apa.org

In the U.K., Europe, Africa, and the Middle East, copies may be ordered from
American Psychological Association
3 Henrietta Street
Covent Garden, London
WC2E 8LU England

Typeset in Trump Medieval by Circle Graphics, Inc., Columbia, MD

Printer: United Book Press, Baltimore, MD
Cover Designer: Naylor Design, Washington, DC

The opinions and statements published are the responsibility of the authors, and such opinions and statements do not necessarily represent the policies of the American Psychological Association.

Library of Congress Cataloging-in-Publication Data

Williams-Nickelson, Carol.
  Internships in psychology : the APAGS workbook for writing successful applications and finding the right fit / Carol Williams-Nickelson, Mitchell J. Prinstein, and W. Gregory Keilin. — 3rd ed.
     p. cm.
  Includes bibliographical references.
  ISBN 978-1-4338-1210-1 — ISBN 1-4338-1210-X 1. Psychology—Study and teaching (Internship)
I. Williams-Nickelson, Carol. II. Prinstein, Mitchell J., 1970- III. Keilin, W. Gregory. IV. Internships in psychology. V. Title.

  BF77.I67 2013
  150.71'55—dc23

                              2012012576

British Library Cataloguing-in-Publication Data
A CIP record is available from the British Library.

Printed in the United States of America
Third Edition

DOI: 10.1037/13946-000

CONTENTS

PREFACE

Not so long ago, few resources were available to help students navigate the internship application process. Students experienced a great deal of anxiety and confusion throughout the process and had many questions about how best to proceed. This great unmet need led the three of us to become involved with local and national associations that advocate for students and attend to training issues. We served on committees, were elected to offices, and were asked to speak at conferences about the internship process. These activities ultimately led to the creation of the first American Psychological Association of Graduate Students (APAGS) special preconvention workshop on the internship application process, which was presented at the 108th Annual Convention of the American Psychological Association (APA) in 2000 in Washington, DC.

We created a set of handouts, which we conceived as a workbook, that were designed to help applicants prepare for each aspect of the internship application process in a careful, systematic manner. We hoped that through the workshop and the workbook, we would help students reconsider the internship application process as an opportunity to consult with advisors, to develop professional goals, to meet dozens of professionals with a range of experiences, and to discuss their professional development and interests with people outside of their graduate program. By reframing the tasks involved in this process, we hoped that the application procedure might become a little less cumbersome and that applicants could focus on finding not just an internship but the right internship for them.

The workshop was a hit, and our hopes for this workbook were more than realized. We have consistently received extraordinary feedback from students. The early versions of this workbook were distributed directly by the APAGS office and were very popular. We were therefore happy when, in 2004, APA Books took over publication of the workbook and gave it even wider distribution. The workbook has been updated regularly to reflect changes in the application process and trends in psychology training and internship availability.

Now in its third APA Books edition, this workbook continues to evolve to reflect the changing application process. Recently, the application process transitioned to an online system. The traditional Clearinghouse has been replaced with a second Match. In addition, the internship marketplace has changed. This edition of the workbook offers updated and enhanced information to address all of these modifications to the application process. A new chapter addressed to directors of clinical training has been added, offering suggestions on how they might best assist students during this process. Numerous additional changes also have been offered—many of which are based on readers' feedback on prior editions.

We are pleased that the workbook is now available to a greater number of students and that APA Books shares our goal of keeping the price low to accommodate students' limited budgets. A portion of the proceeds from this book will again be donated to APAGS to continue supporting programs that directly benefit students. For example, APAGS has presented portions of the internship workshop around the country, and sales of the book have supported many additional APAGS-developed programs that address internship issues as well as other important aspects of graduate training in psychology. It should be noted that we receive no direct financial gain from our work on this project. We are thrilled that students have found this workbook to be an invaluable resource, and we are very pleased to offer this new edition with substantial changes and updates.

Like past editions, this volume has a practical orientation, presenting a discussion of each aspect of the internship process in order. We have included numerous examples to help applicants calculate their clinical hours, compose essays, draft thank-you notes, and practice interview questions. The examples are from real applicants, all of whom successfully obtained an internship match; they are neither ideal nor flawless but are realistic, excellent examples that illustrate many of the suggestions offered in this volume. We are grateful to the brave internship applicants who provided us with their materials to be presented anonymously in this book.

We hope this volume will provide readers the support and assistance they need to successfully navigate the internship application process. It is just one of several services made available to students by APAGS, a group within APA committed to representing, leading, advocating for, and developing resources for psychology graduate students. APAGS and the Association of Psychology Postdoctoral and Internship Centers (APPIC) have developed and continue to cultivate a close relationship so that APAGS can inform APPIC of the needs, concerns, successes, and ideas of internship applicants and so that APPIC can advise APAGS of new programs, improved systems, and other information that is useful for APAGS members negotiating the internship process.

Good luck to you all!

ACKNOWLEDGMENTS

Thanks to you, internship applicants! This workbook was developed to address your needs and was shaped by your feedback and encouragement during our annual American Psychological Association of Graduate Students (APAGS) internship workshops. Your ongoing support and expressions of gratitude have been our inspiration and the motivating force for both completing this project and keeping the content fresh and relevant. Your membership in APAGS has also helped to make our workshop and workbook available to students each year. We hope this workbook offers you some direction, comfort, and perspective, along with a little humor, throughout the internship application process.

We also thank all of the students who voluntarily provided sections of their actual internship application materials for use in this workbook without any expectation of recognition or reward. Their gesture of goodwill and camaraderie is greatly appreciated by APAGS because their work will help future generations of internship applicants.

We also gratefully acknowledge Richard Suinn, past president of the American Psychological Association (APA), and the APA Board of Directors for allocating seed money from their limited contingency funds in 2000 to help launch the workshop and workbook. Nadine J. Kaslow, past chair of the Association of Psychology Postdoctoral and Internship Centers (APPIC), and the entire APPIC board deserve tremendous recognition for their dedication to students and to internship training. We would also like to thank our colleague and good friend Shane J. Lopez for his many contributions to earlier editions of this workbook, for his participation in many of our APA preconvention workshops, for his national leadership on behalf of students and APAGS, and for his enduring good humor.

Carol Williams-Nickelson would like to thank the staff of the University of Notre Dame Counseling Center, especially Sue Steibe-Pasalich, Patrick Utz, Micky Franco, Rita Donley, and Dominic Vachon, for a memorable and richly rewarding internship experience. The immeasurable support provided by her husband, David Nickelson, and her colleagues at APA, particularly L. Michael Honaker, her former supervisor and APA's deputy chief executive officer, is deeply appreciated.

Mitch Prinstein extends unending gratitude to his mentors, Annette La Greca and Tony Spirito, for their career guidance and support, as well as to Audrey Zakriski, Greta Francis, Fran D'Elia, Rod Gragg, and Donn Posner for an excellent internship experience. Mitch also extends thanks to his friends and family for everything, always.

Greg Keilin would like to thank his graduate advisor, Scott Hamilton, and his internship training director, Melba Vasquez, for their support and mentorship throughout the years. He would also like to thank his colleagues on the APPIC Board of Directors, an incredibly energetic and dedicated group of individuals who have been willing to take the bold steps necessary to support quality training and to make the internship selection process more manageable for students.

Internships
in Psychology

1

GETTING STARTED: GENERAL OVERVIEW OF THE INTERNSHIP APPLICATION PROCESS

The psychology internship application process can be rewarding, exhausting, stressful, and exciting. Your internship training marks the beginning of the final stages of your graduate career in professional psychology and is a milestone that you should be proud of reaching. Congratulations!

You have been preparing for internship since your first day of graduate school. As a result, you have acquired many valuable experiences that can make you very attractive to the right internship program. The process of gathering materials, calculating your clinical hours, developing your curriculum vitae (CV), establishing and articulating your internship and career goals, interviewing with various internship sites, being matched to a site that is a good fit, and finally going on internship is one of the most valuable exercises you will undertake as a graduate student. This process will help you review and assess all of your previous training, evaluate your collective graduate experiences, define your training and career goals, practice your job application and interviewing skills, and launch you into professional status as a practitioner.

This chapter provides you with a broad overview of the entire internship application process and gives you some organizational tools to assist you in preparation. It is no secret that decisions about internship often are difficult and anxiety provoking. The process includes many unknown factors that you may be contemplating: "Where will I go? Will I measure up? Will my application be competitive? Do I really have what it takes to make it? Can I move? Will I survive living in a region that has snow? Will my family be supportive? How will I live on the small stipend I am paid? What will my supervisors be like? Will I connect with my fellow interns? What will be next for me after internship? Will I have a positive experience?" As you well know, change is rarely easy and is almost always stressful. We hope to help you to eliminate some of the

DOI: 10.1037/13946-001
Internships in Psychology: The APAGS Workbook for Writing Successful Applications and Finding the Right Fit, Third Edition, by C. Williams-Nickelson, M. J. Prinstein, and W. G. Keilin

unproductive worry you may be experiencing and instead to capitalize on the normal, productive, and motivating anxiety that is a natural part of doing anything new and different, particularly when you are being evaluated.

This chapter begins with an explanation of the purpose of the predoctoral internship, followed by a description of the role of the Association of Psychology Postdoctoral and Internship Centers (APPIC) throughout the selection process. Next, we review the topic of accreditation as it relates to the selection of internship programs and discuss the implications for licensure and future employment if you choose not to attend an accredited internship program.

We then discuss four areas to help you survey and prepare for what is ahead of you in the application process. First, we review internship application milestones that mark the major tasks in the process and help you track your overall progress. We present a sequential checklist that details the major preparatory work you will need to begin now to ensure that you will be able to easily complete your APPIC Application for Psychology Internships (AAPI). We review the *APPIC Directory Online* and discuss developing your strategy for the number of sites and geographic regions to which you may wish to apply. We present data from previous years about the number of sites to which students have applied and their match rates. We also discuss the main reasons why applicants do not match. Finally, we review various psychological approaches to the process and how you can prepare yourself to be open-minded about this next level of your training. So, relax as much as you can, and do your best to learn from and enjoy this process.

The chapter is designed to help you get organized and put things in perspective. We understand that you may be worried about the many nuances of where and how to apply for internships and especially how to present yourself to an entirely new group of faculty and supervisors who will be evaluating you all over again. After all, you have probably already established yourself in your program as a competent student with a variety of talents. Now you are tasked with explaining and showcasing your competence and talents to a new group of evaluators. This is not the first time that you will have to do this, nor will it be the last. Each time you apply for a new job, even if you have a stellar and well-known reputation, you will have to sell yourself and your skills. Preparing for and applying to internship sites is one of the best ways of practicing for future job interviews and opportunities. If you plan and prepare well now, you will gain valuable skills and knowledge that will benefit you for years to come.

THE PREDOCTORAL INTERNSHIP

The psychology predoctoral internship is typically a yearlong, full-time clinical training experience that is a required part of a student's doctoral program. The internship often is described as the "capstone" of graduate training in psychology and differs from practicum and work experience by its rigorous nature, its timing in the overall sequence of graduate training, the intensive supervision and training received, the focus on the development of advanced skills, and the high level of organization and commitment to the training program that is required of the sponsoring agency. Although a very limited number of 2-year, half-time internship positions are available, the vast majority of students attend internship on a full-time basis. The internship typically occurs in the final year of one's doctoral program and ideally after the student has completed comprehensive examinations and proposed (or, it is hoped, defended) his or her dissertation. APPIC policies state that internship applicants must be currently enrolled in a doctoral program in professional psychology (i.e., clinical, counseling, or school psychology) that requires internship training and must have completed practicum experience.

Applicants begin preparing for internship at the beginning of their training program by carefully selecting the type of practicum training they receive and by tracking and recording all related training hours, experiences, and supervision. This process helps prospective interns consider the type of training they still need when it comes time to apply for internship.

ASSOCIATION OF PSYCHOLOGY POSTDOCTORAL AND INTERNSHIP CENTERS

The first step in preparing for internship is to become familiar with APPIC and its website at http://www.appic.org. APPIC is an organization consisting of internship and postdoctoral training programs in the United States and Canada. APPIC oversees the internship selection process by providing resources for students such as the AAPI Online, an online directory of APPIC member internship sites, the APPIC Match, and the Post Match Vacancy Service. APPIC is governed by a board of directors elected by its membership to represent training directors in predoctoral and postdoctoral psychology training programs. Although APPIC is not an accrediting agency, its member programs are required to meet certain criteria to be accepted for membership. Thus, although not as rigorous or as highly regarded as American Psychological Association (APA) and Canadian Psychological Association (CPA) accreditation, a training program that is a member of APPIC has been reviewed and has met specific standards set by that organization. Nearly all of the over 480 internship sites accredited by the APA and CPA are members of APPIC, and an additional 200 nonaccredited programs are members as well.

WHAT IS ACCREDITATION AND WHY IS IT IMPORTANT?

In professional psychology, an internship or doctoral program that is accredited by APA or CPA has achieved the highest form of recognition available. Students who complete APA- or CPA-accredited doctoral and internship programs are least likely to have difficulties in becoming licensed or in securing employment as a psychologist. In fact, some states have begun to institute laws that *require* participation in an APA or CPA accredited internship for licensure. Accreditation by APA and CPA is different from other forms of accreditation (e.g., regional accreditation) because these other forms carry very little weight when it comes to your future as a psychologist. For the purposes of this workbook, the term *accreditation* will refer only to accreditation by APA or CPA.

Accreditation is a voluntary process. It is also rigorous, time consuming, and expensive for the program. Internship programs that apply for accreditation must develop an organized training model along with a sequence of training and clinical experiences that fit that model. They must provide a certain level of supervision, adequate physical resources, and a reasonable stipend. Furthermore, every 5 to 7 years, programs must complete an extensive document called a "Self-Study" (which can be as long as a dissertation!) and host an on-site visit by members of the accrediting body.

So, attending an accredited internship can help you feel confident that you will have a high-quality training experience as well as the comfort of knowing that it is highly unlikely that you will encounter barriers when applying for licensure or employment.

If you are considering attending an unaccredited internship program, it is important that you understand the potential risks in doing so. Although only a few state licensing boards actually require an accredited internship, some states have specific criteria that an unaccredited internship must meet to be licensed in that state. If your internship does not meet those requirements, you will not be able to be licensed (see the Association of State and Provincial Psychology Boards' website, http://www.asppb.org, for more information). As far as future employment is concerned, many employers prefer—and some even require—psychologists who interned at and graduated from

Table 1.1   *Nine-Year Comparison of Match Trends*

	2002	2011	9-year change	
Participating sites	610	690	+80	(+13%)
Positions offered	2,752	3,166	+414	(+15%)
Positions filled	2,410	2,910	+500	(+21%)
Positions unfilled	342	256	−86	(−25%)
Registered applicants	3,073	4,199	+1,126	(+37%)
Withdrawn applicants	231	352	+121	(+52%)
Matched applicants	2,410	2,910	+500	(+21%)
Unmatched applicants	432	937	+505	(+117%)

Note. Data from the 2011 Post-Match Internship Survey. The 2011 numbers reflect activity from Phase I only in order to allow comparisons to the 2002 figures.

accredited programs. Some examples include academic positions and faculty appointments, positions on competitive managed-care panels, and all psychologist positions in Veterans Affairs hospitals and clinics.

INTERNSHIP SUPPLY AND DEMAND

Most applicants have heard about the internship "supply and demand" problem. Over the past decade, there has been an increasing imbalance between the number of students seeking an internship and the number of internship positions available (see Table 1.1). For example, in 2011, the number of applicants who were matched in both phases of the APPIC Match was 3,095, or 79%, whereas the number unmatched to an internship site was 804, or 21%. While an unknown (and probably small) number of these unmatched applicants eventually found a position after the Match, a very significant number of qualified applicants had to delay their internship until the following year.

The good news is that, for those students who did get placed in the 2011 APPIC Match, nearly half were matched to their top-ranked internship program, approximately two thirds received one of their top two choices, and four in five were matched to one of their top three choices.

APPIC conducted a survey in 2011 to assess applicants' beliefs about why they were not matched (see Exhibit 1.1). It is interesting that students did not attribute the lack of a match to any personal characteristics or shortcomings. Although the supply-and-demand problem has definitely left very competent and capable students without internships, dispositional or individual preparedness factors occasionally contribute to students' remaining unmatched.

Exhibit 1.1.   *Unmatched Applicants' Perceptions About Why They Did Not Match*

1. 90%, Imbalance between applicants and positions
2. 39%, Random factors/bad luck
3. 34%, Applied to too many highly competitive sites
4. 31%, Applied to a limited geographic area
5. 21%, Inability to relocate
6. 21%, Bias against my degree type (e.g., PsyD, PhD, EdD)
7. 21%, Not enough sites to apply to in my area of specialization
8. 19%, Applied to too few sites

Note. Data from the 2011 APPIC Survey.

WHY DO PEOPLE REALLY NOT MATCH?

Aside from there being more applicants than available internships, our experience suggests that applicants do not match for the following reasons:

- Applicant is geographically restricted.
- Applicant applies to too few sites (i.e., fewer than 10 sites).
- Applicant applies to primarily "competitive" sites (i.e., sites that receive a large number of applications for a small number of positions).
- Applicant needs to attend a part-time internship (very few are available).
- Applicant is from an unaccredited doctoral program.
- Applicant is not a good fit for the programs to which he or she applies.
- Essays are poorly written or not compelling.
- Interviewing skills are deficient.
- Letters of recommendation are weak.
- Applicant has insufficient clinical experience.
- Applicant displays interpersonal difficulties.

HOW MANY SITES SHOULD YOU APPLY TO?

Each year, many applicants wonder how many internship programs they should apply to in order to maximize their chances of being placed. APPIC's most recent study on this issue was conducted in 2011, when 2,731 applicants (65%) completed a post-Match survey. In this survey, applicants reported submitting an average of 16.0 applications (median = 16, mode = 15) and receiving an average of 6.4 interviews (median = 6, mode = 6). See Table 1.2 for a summary of how well applicants did in the Match over a 3-year period on the basis of the number of applications submitted.

As you can see from this table, applying to more than 15 sites does not appear to improve your chances of being matched. We recommend applying to between 10 and 15 sites, and certainly no more than 15, as staying in this range allows you to keep the number of interviews at a manageable (both emotionally and financially) level.

INTERNSHIP MILESTONES

The internship application process can be long and arduous. Consider the process to be a series of small, manageable tasks. To help you review these tasks and ensure that you stay on track, consult the "Internship Milestones at a Glance" checklist (see Exhibit 1.2) throughout the application process. We encourage you to refer to this list often and record the dates on which you accomplish each milestone.

The more organized you are, the easier it will be to complete your applications and to meet the many overlapping deadlines. The suggested checklist can help you arrange all of your supporting application materials so that, when it is time, you can complete

Table 1.2 *Internship Applicants Who Successfully Matched, on the Basis of the Number of Submitted Applications*

No. of applications submitted	2011 match rate
1–5	62%
6–10	72%
11–15	83%
16–20	81%
21 or more	81%

Note. Data from the 2011 APPIC Post-Match Internship Survey.

Exhibit 1.2. *Internship Milestones at a Glance*

1. Compute practica hours, including anticipated hours.   _____
2. Register for the AAPI Online (APPIC Application for Psychology Internships)   _____
   at http://www.appic.org
3. Use the *APPIC Directory Online* to find sites that match your interests.   _____
   Review each site's Web-based materials or request their materials via e-mail
   or regular mail.
4. Register for the APPIC Match (see the APPIC website).   _____
5. Prepare curriculum vitae.   _____
6. Request letters of recommendation.   _____
7. Draft application essays.   _____
8. Complete the AAPI Online (and any supplemental materials that may be site   _____
   specific) and write individualized cover letters.

9. Begin to schedule interviews.   _____
10. Practice a sample case presentation.   _____
11. Review materials for each site, and decide if you would like to complete   _____
    a literature search on some of the people you will interview with
    (if appropriate).
12. Compose your questions for internship sites.   _____
13. Send thank-you notes/follow-up letters (optional).   _____
14. Submit Rank Order List for the Match before the deadline.   _____

your application with minimal frustration and without scrambling for information. Obtaining and organizing the information you will need to report on the AAPI Online can be a long process, so you need to get started early.

Step 1. Visit the APPIC Website

You should begin the internship application process with a visit to the APPIC website (http://www.appic.org), with a focus on three specific areas:

    1a. *Review the AAPI Online.* Create a new account for the AAPI Online service (there is no charge to do so) and explore the various sections and requirements. Doing so well in advance will provide you with an important head start in terms of understanding the information that you will need to collect and enter into your online application. In fact, it is extremely helpful to maintain a log of your clinical experiences beginning with your very first (i.e., first- or second-year) graduate school practicum experience, as the AAPI Online asks for very extensive information (e.g., treatment setting, type of intervention, client demographics) about those experiences.

    1b. *Search the APPIC Directory.* Most students find that the *APPIC Directory Online* is their most useful source of information on internship programs, as it lists the nearly 700 internship programs that are current APPIC members. The *APPIC Directory Online* is updated regularly by internship training directors and provides excellent search capabilities. Entering a set of search parameters and clicking the "Search" button will yield a list of internship programs that match your criteria. You may then click on any internship program in that list to display more information about that specific program. Note that a few APA divisions also maintain their own internship directories for programs that fit a specific area of interest (e.g., clinical neuropsychology; science-oriented internship programs) that are available online as well.

Here are some tips on getting the most out of searching the *APPIC Directory Online*:

- You may specify as many or as few search parameters as you wish. Increasing the number of search parameters used generally decreases the number of internship programs returned by the search.
- You may find it useful to search for internships that indicate that they accept applicants from your specific type of graduate program (e.g., school psychology, EdD programs).
- If you are looking for half-time, 2-year internships, use the "part-time" search option to locate such programs. Keep in mind that the number of available half-time internship positions tends to be very limited.
- You can search for any of the 60 "Training Opportunities" listed. For example, you could search for all programs that serve a Spanish-speaking population, conduct cognitive rehabilitation, or specialize in child neuropsychology.
- You will find that each program's listing includes directions on how to obtain additional information about the program and its application requirements (most programs have either a website or a printed brochure available).
- You can use the "bookmark" feature in your web browser to save any search result for future reference.

In addition to the *APPIC Directory Online*, faculty members and fellow graduate students are often excellent sources of information about internships. Contacting students from your program who are currently on internship or who have recently completed an internship may allow you to benefit from their internship search experiences. In addition, faculty will often know of internship programs that have had positive experiences with other students from your program and thus may be particularly welcoming of your application.

For students who are looking for internships in California, the California Psychology Internship Council (see http://www.capic.net) publishes a directory of internship programs in that state. Most of these programs are neither APA-accredited nor members of APPIC, and most do not participate in the APPIC Match. Many are unpaid experiences. In addition, the positions at these sites are generally filled by students who are enrolled in doctoral programs in California.

1c. *Subscribe to the MATCH-NEWS E-Mail List.* This list provides news, tips, and information directly from APPIC about the selection process and the Match. It is strongly recommended that you subscribe to MATCH-NEWS very early in the process, as the information provided can be very helpful. MATCH-NEWS is a low-volume list, usually sending no more than five e-mail messages per month, and thus you will not be inundated with e-mail.

Step 2. Get More Information About Each Site

Once you have reviewed the information in the *APPIC Directory Online*, you should obtain as much information as possible about the sites in which you are interested. Most sites now have their internship information available on their websites, but a few still require you to send them a simple e-mail, postcard, or letter to request their printed materials. Review each site's materials to determine whether you are a good fit for their training program. This can sometimes be difficult, as many sites sound quite similar in their written materials. It may be helpful to review each site with your specific goals in mind (see Chapter 3 for a discussion on constructing goals for internship training).

As you review the materials for each site of interest, it may be helpful to record some specific information for each site. The "sample summary sheet" in Exhibit 1.3 is one example of how you might track and organize that information. In particular:

- Make a note of the application deadline for each site in which you are interested. Application deadlines vary and are easily missed if you are not careful.
- Make a note of any special eligibility or application requirements.
- In addition to tracking deadlines and application requirements, you should make notes about the aspects of each program that excite you and/or for which you are a particularly good fit (based on your background, interests, and experiences). You should also note any aspects of the programs that are "negatives" or a poor fit for what you are seeking, or areas in which you have questions or need more information. Recording this information at this stage will make it easier for you to make decisions about where to apply and will also help you write a compelling cover letter for each program when you get to that stage of the process.

Step 3. Decide Where to Apply

Once you have gathered and reviewed the information about each program, you will need to make some decisions about where you wish to apply. Here are some suggestions:

- Carefully review the summary sheets that you created and rate your level of interest in each site. You may note that a site that initially appeared quite exciting became less so as you reviewed other sites, or vice versa.

Exhibit 1.3.   *Sample Summary Sheet of Application Site Requirements*

Name of site:
Application deadline:
Site-specific application requirements:
Specific programs or rotations of interest:
Strengths of this program:
Weaknesses of this program:
Quality of fit:
Ideas about areas to highlight in cover letter:
Questions to ask:
Overall interest: 1   2   3   4   5
Notes:

- Review your site interests and preferences with your mentor or a trusted faculty member for his or her input and impressions. You may also wish to consult with your director of clinical training (DCT) and/or students from your program who have recently completed the application process. Such conversations may have an impact on your level of interest in some sites.
- Order the summary sheets from highest to lowest interest. Use this organizational mechanism to determine the sites to which you will apply. Limit your choices to no more than 15 sites.
- Begin gathering and organizing all of the information that you will need (e.g., clinical hours, testing experience) to report on your applications (see Chapter 2 for more information on the AAPI Online).
- Begin collecting the materials necessary to complete your CV (e.g., dates of training, clinical supervisors' names, titles and authors for presentations or publications).
- Order one official copy of your transcript from each school or university at which you completed graduate-level work (regardless of whether or not you received a graduate degree), sent by the school directly to the AAPI Online service. You should *not* order or send undergraduate transcripts to the AAPI Online service.
- Identify three people whom you would like to ask to write your recommendation letters. Three letters are usually required by each site.
- Make appointments and talk with these three potential references, asking *directly* as to whether they would feel comfortable writing you strong letters of recommendation in support of your internship search.
- Provide each reference with a copy of your CV, essays, goals for internship, summary of your strengths and areas to highlight, and other important information that will make their letter writing as easy as possible. Do not wait until the last minute to do this, and do not do this too far in advance—to prevent a rush job or a forgotten job.

Step 4. Develop a Helpful Mind-Set

As we have informally talked with, advised, and consoled students preparing for internship, four applicant mind-sets have consistently emerged as common psychological approaches to the internship process. Some people may consider these as stress-management strategies, coping processes, defense mechanisms, heuristics, unconscious slips, or socially constructed narratives. Whatever you choose to call them, you will undoubtedly identify with some of these cognitions and perhaps even notice them in your peers.

The following taxonomy of themes seems to capture the beliefs of most students preparing to apply for internship. As you review them, see whether your thinking matches any of these common beliefs and, if so, whether you are comfortable with your approach or whether it might be helpful to make some cognitive shifts.

The "Just do it!" mind-set. This mind-set is characterized by one or more of the following thoughts and beliefs:

- "Internship is just another hoop that I have to jump through to get my degree and get on with my life."
- "Internship isn't that important in the grand scheme of things, anyway."

- "I'll just do it and get it over with in the most painless way possible."
- "I'll take anything, anywhere, whatever I can get—because I can endure anything for one year."

The "I'm too prepared and talented for them" mind-set. This approach is characterized by one or more of the following thoughts and beliefs:

- "My practicum experiences were outstanding—probably the best in the country. I deserve to be a psychologist *now*. I don't want or need to do an internship."
- "My program was so fabulous; there couldn't possibly be anything else an internship site can teach me."
- "This is one of those easy sites. This year will be a breeze."
- "I'm smarter than most of the internship faculty at this site!"

The "This decision will determine my life course" mind-set. This mind-set is characterized by one or more of the following thoughts and beliefs:

- "Selecting an internship site is one of the most important decisions I'll ever make in my life."
- "My internship will either open up endless possibilities for my career or stifle my career forever."

The "I acknowledge reciprocity" mind-set. This approach is characterized by the following thought and belief:

- "This internship will present me with opportunities to enhance and refine my skills, and I have some talents and ideas that will benefit the site."

How does your current mind-set compare to the beliefs presented here? If you most closely identify with the first three mind-sets, you probably need an intervention . . . and fast! If your thoughts most closely match the reciprocity mind-set, you are on the right track (even if you struggle with some of the others some of the time), and you are likely to become more actualized as you learn more about the process. Clearly, the most grounded and useful stance to take is one that recognizes the interdependence between the intern and the trainers. The promotion of mutuality creates an atmosphere of respect, curiosity, and shared inquiry. It is important for you to realize that not only are you academically prepared to contribute in meaningful ways and expand your knowledge, you also bring your unique life experiences, personality, and perspectives to the training program. This is highly valued by sites and supervisors. In addition, you also will have some wonderful opportunities to be exposed to new people, along with new ways of thinking and doing things that will enhance your skills as an emerging practitioner if you choose to take advantage of them. In the end, regardless of how you classify your thoughts, the information that follows in this book will help you become better prepared, more poised, and well positioned. We hope that you will be able to present yourself as you intend.

THE NEXT STEP   Now that you have a grasp on the overarching tasks that you will need to accomplish in the internship application process, it is time to turn your attention to the actual application. Chapter 2 presents the elements of the application and provides some suggestions and overarching principles for completing the process.

2

COMPLETING THE APPIC APPLICATION FOR PSYCHOLOGY INTERNSHIPS

After glancing over the long Association of Psychology Postdoctoral and Internship Centers (APPIC) Application for Psychology Internships (AAPI), you may see the job of completing the application as daunting. Keeping track of all your clinical tasks, such as counting and recording each hour of therapy, supervision, group work, assessment, test interpretation, and consultation, while recording the age, ethnicity, and diversity status of your clients, can be overwhelming. But it need not be if you break the tasks of gathering information and completing the AAPI into manageable pieces.

This chapter can help you do exactly that. It offers practical guidance and suggestions for completing the application and walks you through a simple example of how to translate clinical hours to the AAPI. This chapter helps you take a detailed inventory of your clinical skills and experiences. However, bear in mind that there is no single correct method for calculating and recording your hours. Several overarching principles are offered to guide you through completing the AAPI in a way that fairly and accurately represents your training history. The chapter includes a few samples of tables and worksheets that can be modified to suit your needs for organizing and tallying your own clinical hours and related experiences. (Many programs provide students with similar worksheets at the beginning of practicum, and the "Training Resources" section of the APPIC website includes practicum hours tracking spreadsheets that you may find useful.)

WHAT IS THE APPIC APPLICATION FOR PSYCHOLOGY INTERNSHIPS?

Many years ago, before a standard application form was developed, each internship program developed its own unique application form. There was considerable variability in the style of the applications, in the format for recording hours and experiences, and in the manner in which essay questions were posed. Thus, applicants had to devote a tremendous amount of time to completing many lengthy application forms.

DOI: 10.1037/13946-002
Internships in Psychology: The APAGS Workbook for Writing Successful Applications and Finding the Right Fit, Third Edition, by C. Williams-Nickelson, M. J. Prinstein, and W. G. Keilin

In the late 1990s, the AAPI was created by APPIC to make the process more efficient for applicants, to reduce applicant stress, and to create some standardization in the information sought by APPIC-member internship programs. At that time, the AAPI was provided as a template that students would download via the Internet and complete using a word processing program. Although this standardized application resulted in a huge saving of time for applicants, it still meant that applicants had to print each application form, gather the associated materials on paper (i.e., cover letter, letters of recommendation, transcripts), and mail this large packet to each internship site.

In 2009, APPIC took the next step and introduced an online version of the AAPI, called the "AAPI Online" service. This new service allows students to create and submit their applications and all supporting materials directly to internship sites via the Internet, and individuals who provide letters of recommendation can upload those letters directly into the service. Furthermore, applicants submit only one copy of their official graduate transcripts to the AAPI Online service. While the AAPI Online does require applicants to pay a fee to use the service, this fee is more than covered by the cost savings involved in not having to print and mail applications or obtain multiple copies of official transcripts.

The AAPI Online is updated and revised almost every year. While the changes usually aren't major, the AAPI Online is refined each year to better meet the needs of applicants and to provide the information that internship programs find most important and helpful. It is very important to review the AAPI Online as soon as it becomes available (usually in July) so that you have time to gather the necessary data to complete it.

Keep in mind that although the AAPI is very important, it is only part of a series of items and information that will be used to evaluate your potential to succeed and your fit with a particular site. Referring to the major tasks you will need to accomplish in the internship application process, outlined earlier in Exhibit 1.2, you will notice that completing the AAPI is the eighth in a series of 14 steps or milestones. Keeping the internship tasks in perspective throughout the application process can help you maintain a grounded mind-set.

The elements that make up a completed application are as follows (please note that more information about many of these elements is provided in later chapters of this workbook):

1. The "core" part of your application, including contact information, educational background, current graduate program, professional conduct, and a summary of your practicum experience.
2. A cover letter. We strongly recommend submitting a different cover letter to each site.
3. A curriculum vitae (CV). You may use the same CV for all sites to which you apply, or you may upload multiple versions and choose the version that is submitted to each site.
4. Responses to four essay questions. You may use the same essays for all sites or you may create multiple versions.
5. Certification by your director of clinical training (DCT). Once you have completed the "Summary of Doctoral Training" portion of your application, you must submit that section to your DCT for review and verification. In addition to verifying the information that you included in that section, the DCT will be asked to provide evaluative information about your progress in the program and certify your readiness for internship. In the event that your DCT doesn't agree

with the information you provided in that section, he or she may return it to you for modification. Once you submit this section to your DCT, it is locked, and further changes will not be permitted. Thus, you should very carefully review your application for errors or omissions before submitting it to your DCT.

6. Letters of reference. The AAPI Online requires each of your references to upload their letters of recommendation directly into the service. Once someone has agreed to serve as a reference, you may use the "References" section of the AAPI Online to submit a formal invitation to that individual. This invitation is delivered in the form of an e-mail message that provides the reference with detailed instructions about how to upload the letter. Most sites ask for three letters of recommendation, and most applicants send the same three letters to all sites to which they are applying. However, it is acceptable to (a) ask for more than three people to serve as references in order to send different letters to different sites, and/or (b) have a single reference write multiple versions of his or her letter. You should be judicious about using either of these options and do so only when sending different versions of letters to different sites is really necessary (e.g., if you are applying to very different settings or types of sites that might call for different things to be emphasized in each letter). Consult with your advisor and/or references if you aren't sure of the best approach.

7. Supplemental materials. Some internship sites ask applicants to submit additional site-specific information with their applications, such as testing or clinical reports or summaries, additional essay questions, or copies of undergraduate transcripts.

The remainder of this chapter provides general information on completing the AAPI Online as well as information about how to record your practicum experiences. Chapter 3 provides detailed information about identifying your goals, writing cover letters, and answering the essay questions, while Chapter 4 discusses CVs, recommendation letters, and supplemental materials.

COMPLETING THE AAPI

Before you can complete the AAPI, you need to obtain and organize the information that will be reported on it. Calculating hours and determining the most appropriate categories for recording certain hours is idiosyncratic and ultimately up to you and your DCT to negotiate and verify. Students often have a lot of anxiety around the number of direct service hours they think they should have, and they look for prescribed information or precise formulas for structuring their clinical experiences so they can meet these mythical criteria or quotas. As a rule, always consult your DCT if you have any uncertainties about what clinical experiences you may count as direct service hours or how to record particular training activities.

What follows are general principles and tips—some dos and don'ts—that will help you organize your approach to the AAPI:

- *Do* visit the APPIC website (http://www.appic.org) to review the general AAPI Online instructions along with the "Frequently Asked Questions."
- *Do* read the instructions that are contained within each section of the AAPI Online service. These instructions are quite comprehensive and will answer many of your questions.

- *Don't* send each site the exact same cover letter. For each site to which you apply, it is *essential* that your cover letter address the unique aspects of the site that interest you, and that you discuss why your interests, background, and experiences are a great fit for that site.
- *Don't* assume that the person reviewing your application knows all about you and your program. Applicants often omit training details that are assumed by the applicant to be universal but actually are unique and important for the internship site to know.
- *Don't* tally all of your hours from logs, calendars, or loose sheets of paper just before sitting down to complete the AAPI. Develop an organized record-keeping system with cumulative totals early in your training. You will need to know many details about the setting, age, gender, ethnicity, diversity status, and type of direct service provided at each practicum site. Start recording these details during your first practicum.
- *Do* organize and review your practica log sheets for accuracy and clarity before completing the AAPI. A mathematical error early on can take hours to find down the road.
- *Don't* count all of your learning experiences as bona fide practica hours. For example, practicing the administration of a test on your partner or a classmate and participating in mock sessions as class demonstrations do not count as practicum hours.
- *Do* be honest in reporting your hours and experiences.
- *Don't* become obsessive or paranoid about ensuring that every fraction of an hour is reported accurately and reflected in the proper category!
- *Do* ask your DCT all of your "Can I count . . . ?" questions about reporting your practicum hours. Your DCT is ultimately responsible for verifying that your practicum hours are appropriate and supervised. You are responsible for knowing (and reporting) that practicum hours are those obtained: (a) by practicing your skills; (b) under appropriate supervision; (c) as part of an organized, sequential training experience; (d) with real clients; and (e) in real treatment settings.
- *Do* use your best judgment and realize that you will not be brought up on ethics charges if you make a benign mistake.
- *Don't* inflate your numbers or experiences to try to make you appear more compatible with a particular site.
- *Don't* misrepresent yourself.
- *Do* remember that you are going on internship to learn. This will help reduce feelings of inadequacy as you notice how many blank spaces you are leaving on your application.
- *Do* read the AAPI instructions and follow them. (But *don't* read between the lines, because there is nothing hidden there.) Every attempt has been made to ensure that the instructions are clear, but if you become confused or have an unusual situation, consult with others to determine the best method for reporting your experience.
- *Don't* submit your AAPI without having it reviewed and edited by your peers and faculty.
- *Do* edit your AAPI on more than one occasion and over a period of time.

- *Do* use the "Save" feature frequently as you are completing the AAPI Online. In particular, don't navigate away from any page or section without first saving your work.
- *Don't* violate Match policies. Simply do not "communicate, solicit, accept, or use any ranking-related information prior to the release of the match results" as outlined in the APPIC rules.
- *Do* ask individuals who will be providing letters of recommendation, "Can you write a letter of strong support?" *Don't* press someone to write a recommendation who articulates any reservations or shows any hesitancy to your request. Unusually vague or bad letters of recommendation can damage your chances of being matched to an internship.
- *Do* carefully consider the type of autobiographical information you provide in your essays. Pay attention to your reasons for sharing sensitive information such as your ethnic heritage, age, relationship status, socioeconomic status, sexuality, family obligations, visible or invisible disability, and gender. Sometimes, sharing this information can increase your chances for being highly ranked because the program seeks and respects diversity and wants to know about who you are as a person. Other times, this information may be interpreted as indicative of loose boundaries or too much personal disclosure. The best approach is to share what you determine to be most congruent with who you are, what you want to convey about yourself, and what you value in your approach to clinical work and supervision.
- *Don't* write an autobiographical statement that suggests severe psychopathology. It may not be appropriate to share information about your own psychiatric hospitalizations or that you selected psychology as a career because you wanted to learn more about your own disorders!
- *Do* remember that this is an evaluative process, and sites are using this information not only to determine your clinical talent and fit with their training philosophy and opportunities but also to decide whether you are someone who is relatively healthy mentally and someone whom they will enjoy working with for a year or more.
- *Do* contact APPIC if you have difficulties with completing or submitting your applications or if you have questions that aren't answered in the instructions or by your DCT. APPIC has a contact person who is available to address questions or hear your feedback about the AAPI Online; his or her name is listed in the "Contact" section of the APPIC website. If you are experiencing technical problems with the AAPI Online service, such as logging in or submitting applications or transcripts, you may contact the AAPI Online technical support team at support@appicas.org or (617) 612-2899.
- *Do* use the APPIC INTERN-NETWORK e-mail discussion list, as it is a good resource for obtaining opinions about how to record your clinical experiences on the AAPI. A large number of current and former internship applicants, current interns, internship and doctoral training directors, American Psychological Association of Graduate Students (APAGS) leaders, and APPIC board members subscribe to this list and are interested in supporting you through the process. Please note that the INTERN-NETWORK discussion list is separate from the MATCH-NEWS list (described earlier). However, if hearing others' concerns, questions, and anxieties about the process will increase your own distress, stay far away from the INTERN-NETWORK list!

Calculating hours and recording them on the AAPI is one of the most tedious aspects of the application process. There are as many questions about how to count your hours as there are students applying for internship. There is no universally approved or pre-eminent method for counting and recording your hours on the AAPI. Talk with your DCT to determine if you can include certain hours as program-sanctioned experiences. You also may want to consider establishing regular meetings with classmates who are applying for internship so that you can complete your applications together and discuss questions and concerns about documenting your hours.

You are not expected to have experience in all, or even most, of the areas listed on the AAPI. A comprehensive list of possible clinical activities is provided so that applicants may easily complete the application, but this in no way implies that those are experiences that you are expected to have had. Be sure to keep this in mind as you notice that there are many categories that you will leave blank. Blanks do not imply a deficiency in your training or areas that you should immediately seek experience in; rather, they indicate that the particular training may not be relevant to you or the site, or they may show that you are trainable in certain areas, which some sites find appealing.

If you have not done so already, you should immediately begin to develop an organized system for recording your practicum hours as you are accumulating them. This documentation might also be useful to you after internship as you apply for licensure in a particular jurisdiction. Whatever system or form you use for recording hours, be sure to also include all of the demographic information called for on the AAPI, including treatment settings; type of service provided; and client age, gender, ethnicity, disability, and diversity status. In addition, you will need to separate hours that you accumulated as a doctoral student from those that you earned as part of a terminal master's degree. Hours accumulated while earning a master's degree that was part of a doctoral program should be counted as doctoral practicum hours.

If in doubt about how to categorize certain practicum hours, keep in mind that there is often no "right" answer and that some experiences could reasonably be categorized in different ways. Often, you will need to use your best judgment. If you aren't sure where to categorize certain hours or experiences, use the following approach:

1. Be honest and reasonable.
2. Consult the AAPI Online instructions or FAQs.
3. In the face of ambiguity, use your best judgment.
4. If in doubt: Consult with your DCT.
5. If still in doubt: Contact the AAPI online coordinator (contact information is on the AAPI website under "Contact").

There are five main categories in which you will record and summarize your practicum experiences. The first, *Intervention Experience*, includes the following activities:

- individual, group, family and couples therapy;
- career counseling;
- school counseling;
- other interventions, such as intake interviews, substance abuse interventions, consultation, and sports psychology; and

- experiences with students and organizations, such as supervision provided to other students, program development and outreach, outcome assessment, and systems interventions.

The second category, *Psychological Assessment Experience*, includes:

- psychological assessment experience (including psychodiagnostic test administration and neuropsychological assessment);
- a summary of your experiences with adult, adolescent, and child assessment instruments; and
- the number of adult and child/adolescent integrated reports that you have written.

The third category, *Supervision Received*, asks you to summarize the supervision that you have received in both individual and group formats from licensed psychologists, licensed allied mental health professionals, and by others (e.g., advanced graduate students). You are also asked to indicate whether you have made audio or video recordings that were reviewed by a supervisor, and if you have ever been directly observed by a supervisor.

The fourth category, *Additional Information About Practicum Experiences*, asks you to categorize your practicum experiences by treatment setting (e.g., community mental health center, forensic setting, inpatient psychiatric facility) and by certain client variables (race/ethnicity, gender, disability status, and sexual orientation). In addition, you are asked to designate your group therapy experience, your theoretical orientation, and a summary of your nonpracticum clinical work experience.

The final category, *Support Activities*, provides you with an opportunity to describe and quantify those experiences outside of your direct intervention, assessment, and supervision hours that are still focused on the client. These activities include chart review, writing notes, consulting with others about cases, video or audio review, planning one's interventions, assessment interpretation and report writing, didactic training (e.g., seminars, grand rounds), etc.

Be sure to follow the AAPI instructions for further clarification about what constitutes a practicum hour and how to record them. In short, hours must

- have been accrued through November 1 (another section of the AAPI allows you to summarize and describe any anticipated practicum experiences that will occur after November 1 and prior to the beginning of your internship),
- have been a part of formal academic training/credit or sanctioned by your graduate program,
- have been supervised,
- be listed separately for those acquired as part of your master's degree training and those acquired as part of your doctoral training,
- be calculated by actual hours (although a 50-minute session = 1 practicum hour), and
- be counted only once (i.e., the same hour cannot be recorded or counted in different categories, with the exception of the "Additional Information About Practicum Experiences" section). When you have an hour that falls under more than one area, select the one category that you feel best captures the experience. For example, a stress-management group may be counted as a group therapy hour or as a medical/health-related intervention, but not both.

The AAPI also asks for the number of different individuals, groups, families, and couples to whom you have provided services. For example, if you ran a group with 12 individuals in it for 10 weeks, you would record the number "1" in the "Number of different groups" category.

Some graduate students may have excellent clinical experiences that were acquired as part of their work history or volunteer service activities. Because this type of experience is not program-sanctioned or supervised, it cannot be included with your practicum hours. However, the AAPI does include a section in which students may describe these other work-related or volunteer activities. Similarly, students also may describe their teaching experiences.

In the "Psychological Assessment Experience" section, you may list your experience with a variety of testing instruments. The AAPI provides a list of the more common assessment instruments, and you may add any others that you have used that are not included on that list. For each assessment instrument, you are asked to designate the number that you administered and scored, the number of reports that you wrote that included that measure, and the number that you administered as part of a research project.

A separate section for "Integrated Reports" allows you to indicate the number of comprehensive psychological reports that you wrote. Be sure to check the definition of "integrated report" as described in the AAPI Online instructions.

<table>
<tr><td>SUBMITTING YOUR
APPLICATIONS</td><td>Your application is ready to submit to internship sites once all of the following have been completed:</td></tr>
</table>

1. you have entered all information into the AAPI Online and checked it carefully for accuracy,
2. your DCT has successfully verified the "Summary of Doctoral Training" section,
3. your references have written and uploaded your letters of recommendation,
4. the AAPI Online service has received and properly processed your graduate-level transcripts, and
5. you have uploaded your CV, essays, cover letters, and supplemental materials (if needed).

You do not need to submit all of your applications at one time. Be sure to pay close attention to application deadline dates, as each site establishes its own deadline and many are unwilling to accept late applications. For peace of mind, it is recommended that you submit each application no later than 72 hours before the application deadline, just in case technical problems or other issues interfere with the submission process.

To submit an application, you must first "designate" the site to which you are submitting. The term *designations*, as used within the AAPI Online, simply means the internship sites to which you are applying. As you designate a site, you will have the opportunity to indicate the cover letter, CV, letters of recommendation, essays, and supplemental materials you wish to send to that site along with the core application. In the event that a site offers multiple rotations or "programs" (e.g., a neuropsychology rotation, an outpatient rotation), you may designate the programs to which you are applying. Then, once you pay the application fee and finalize the submission, your application will instantly be electronically delivered to the site.

SUMMARY   Calculating your clinical hours and experiences is not usually a fun process; it can be frustrating and confusing even for the most organized individual. However, this task must be accomplished to complete the AAPI and to demonstrate to prospective sites that you have accumulated valuable experiences that make you a good fit for their training opportunities. It is important to start the process of organizing and recording your hours as soon as you begin your practicum. Good documentation will help you easily and swiftly transfer your direct service hours, testing/assessment experience, and client demographic information to the AAPI. If you have questions about the types of hours that you may count or where to include certain hours on your AAPI, you should always consult with your DCT. Remember, there are no absolute answers regarding how you count and record your clinical experiences. Because of this, working closely with your DCT and simply using your best judgment are critical.

After recording your hours, you are ready to begin thinking about your internship and career goals and how to clearly articulate them in your essays. You now have a good sense of where your training gaps exist and what clinical areas are of interest to you. In the next chapter, we walk you through the process of identifying goals and writing essays that reflect who you are and the best type of training environment for your internship year.

3   Goals, Essays, and the Cover Letter

Setting Goals

Many students embarking on the internship application process have established a clear and determined goal: to get a match. This indeed is an important goal, but it is perhaps not entirely sufficient to help you successfully find a training experience that will allow you to fulfill your dreams as a psychologist. In this chapter, we briefly discuss the importance of setting training goals and the manner in which doing so will help you to craft exceptional essays. We also discuss each essay in detail and provide examples and suggestions for mastering this part of the process.

Remember many years ago when you thought it would be fun and interesting to earn a doctoral degree in clinical, counseling, or school psychology? At that time, you may have had some ideas about what you wanted to do professionally after graduation. Perhaps you dreamt of starting a private practice or working in a medical setting, a counseling center, or a secondary school or as a professor in academia. If you are like most graduate students, you probably have spent the last 3 to 6 years or more working on very specific deadlines for classes, clients, theses, and comprehensive exams, and it has been somewhat difficult to take a step back and think about what the ultimate goal of training would be. In fact, many graduate students are more confused about their career goals at this late stage in training than they were when they were first accepted for doctoral study!

Fear not! You will have a career, and it will be worth all of your training! But first, you need to make sure that you have charted a course that will help you to be best prepared for whatever career path you choose. This is why, before you dive into essay writing, it is absolutely essential that you develop a clear set of training goals for internship. Doing so will help make this process transcend being just another training "hoop"

DOI: 10.1037/13946-003

Internships in Psychology: The APAGS Workbook for Writing Successful Applications and Finding the Right Fit, Third Edition, by C. Williams-Nickelson, M. J. Prinstein, and W. G. Keilin
Copyright © 2013 by the American Psychological Association. All rights reserved.

that you must accomplish and instead become a time of introspection, professional growth, and maturity as an independent psychologist. Once you have a clear sense of your goals, you also will be surprised by how much easier it is to write your essays and to respond to interview questions later in this process. In short, goals are the ingredient that separates the more focused, mature, thoughtful, and deliberate applicant from the others, and they are the ingredient that can help to ensure that your internship experience is the best possible fit for you.

Setting goals is a collaborative process that results from discussion with your advisor, clinical supervisors, other students, and perhaps your training director. You may want to schedule some meetings to have frank discussions about your own strengths and weaknesses, as well as the strengths and weaknesses of your training program. Take careful notes of these discussions, and think about your own experiences of when you felt most or least comfortable during your training. You soon will have to make a decision to be in a particular type of setting for a full year, engaging in some very specific clinical and training activities. It will be important that such an experience will help you to feel competent and happy and will contribute to your growth as a psychologist-in-training.

It also will be important to think quite seriously about potential long-term plans for your career. This is perhaps the most difficult part of the process. Once you have finished your interviews, you will have been exposed to a variety of settings in which psychologists practice and to multiple models of careers in psychology. This exposure usually assists in achieving greater clarity of long-term career options. But at this stage of the application process, it may be better to think more about careers that you would rule out rather than those you would "rule in." It is likely that you already know that there are some activities (e.g., therapy, assessment, research, teaching) that you most certainly will want to engage in during your career in large proportion and other activities that you would prefer to minimize. Next, think about what expertise will help you most in achieving such a career. For example, students who wish to enter private practice should be very comfortable with efficacious treatment for the most common presentations of psychopathology in an outpatient setting (e.g., for adults: depression, anxiety, Axis II; for youth: attention-deficit/hyperactivity disorder and oppositional defiant disorder). Students who wish to teach may want to obtain broad exposure to severe psychopathology to assist them in developing lectures on the breadth of psychological symptoms. Students who wish to work in a medical setting likely will want exposure to such an environment and will want to participate on multidisciplinary teams of health care professionals. There likely are specific areas of your expertise (e.g., modalities of treatment, diagnoses, assessment of treatment techniques) that you would like to further develop as a specialty, and thus you may wish to seek focused, intensive training experiences in these areas.

Consider that your internship may be the last focused, intensive training experience in your career. Some students will obtain a postdoctoral fellowship after internship; however, in many cases this experience will be highly specialized. Thus, your internship truly is an opportunity to get broad exposure and intensive training as a student.

In short, it will be important to consider the following:

1. Given my accrued experiences and areas of emerging competency to date, what are the most essential experiences that I need to obtain to become a _____ (insert range of potential career objectives here)?

2. By the time I am a licensed, independent psychologist, I would like to feel that I am competent and autonomous in _____ (insert specific skill/ knowledge domain here).

3. I could probably function somewhat independently in a few areas right now, but I feel that I should get more experience doing _____ (insert specific activity here) before I could feel confident as a psychologist.

It may be helpful to use the worksheet in Exhibit 3.1 to organize your thoughts about your goals.

Exhibit 3.1.   *Goals Worksheet*

It is important for you to be able to clearly articulate your short- and long-term training and career goals. To do this, you should begin to take inventory now. It is always good to write your ideas down on paper so that you can revisit and revise them regularly.

1. I have a lot of experience in:

2. I am lacking experience in:

3. My supervisors suggest that I should learn more about:

4. Do I want a generalist or specialty experience on internship? Why? My goals for internship are:

   1.

   2.

   3.

My short-term career goals are:

1.

2.

3.

My longer term career goals are:

1.

2.

3.

It is hoped that by the time you are done with this process, you will have generated two to four specific training goals for internship. These goals may be somewhat precise, referring to specific experiences, populations, modalities, or activities that you desire for internship training. It is important that you feel that you could justify each one of these goals (i.e., explain why you have selected this training goal in particular), and these training goals should distinguish you as a unique applicant.

(continues)

Exhibit 3.1. *(Continued)*

The following are examples of specific training goals that may help prompt the development of your own goals:

1. I would like to get more experience with behavioral treatments for ADHD.
2. I would like more exposure to severe psychopathology, including psychopathy, in a forensic setting.
3. I would like more experience conducting family therapy (or group therapy, or assessments to diagnose a specific disorder, etc.).
4. I would like to conduct research while on internship and to be exposed to scientist–practitioner careers.
5. I would like to learn more about the counseling center environment and develop expertise with young adults' difficulties.
6. I would like to establish a career and professional network in the Anchorage area.
7. I would like to go to a site that will allow for postdoctoral training.

The following are examples of less specific goals that, by themselves, do not successfully differentiate applicants because they are too vague and lack depth and evidence of introspection:

1. I would like to conduct outpatient treatment with adults.
2. I would like to attend a prestigious site.
3. I would like to become a competent psychologist in the area of assessment.
4. I hope to enjoy my experience on internship by working in many different areas.
5. I am excited about internship and see a large range of possibilities at your site.

GUIDELINES FOR WRITING ESSAYS

Now that you have your goals, you are ready to write your essays! The composition of four brief essays would not seem likely to take a long time, and yet it most certainly does. You may go through many drafts, and you should solicit feedback from many sources. After several drafts, you may find it difficult to read your own work objectively or to retain the ability to scrutinize your work as carefully as you might review an unfamiliar piece of writing. For these reasons, it is very important to allow ample time to construct your essays. This is the only piece of the application process that is still under your control. You already have accrued your practicum experiences, and your letter writers already have formed impressions of your skills. These essays are an excellent opportunity for you to help the reader of your application understand the story and the person that is "between the lines" of your curriculum vitae (CV) and the objective APPIC Application for Psychology Internships (AAPI) information. It is worth substantial effort to ensure that your essays convey your experiences, ideas, reflections, and personality in an accurate and compelling way. This will take some time.

One reason why the essays may be so difficult to write is that they require a different writing style from the type of writing that was required of you during graduate training (i.e., for theses and clinical reports). This writing is in the first person, and you very much want your "voice" to be prominent in the text. This is not to say that you should write informally or use slang, but it also is not necessary for you to demonstrate your high GRE verbal score with the pretentious use of fancy vocabulary. Be yourself, assuming that you indeed are an intelligent, educated, conscientious student who is about to become a learned professional in society.

It is extremely important to remember that your essays will be read by members of admissions committees who have read dozens of others' essays in the same sitting. Thus, clarity is paramount. Short, pithy sentences with simple ideas often work best. You will have spent hours crafting these documents; the ideas within them need to be extremely clear to a reader who will spend a mere minute or two on each one. Few will go back to reread confusing sentences, and even fewer will shuffle between your essays to capture the continuity of your ideas or implicit, subtle themes. You must be explicit in what you are attempting to convey, and you should expect to be repetitive in your main messages.

Your essays should accomplish several objectives. First, you want to offer a genuine reflection of your aspirations for internship training. Honesty is essential to ensure that you not only get a match but that you also get matched to a site that is best for you. Getting matched to a site that is a poor fit for you will lead to a very unhappy year that will compromise your training experiences and undermine your confidence and competence. Do not write essays that say what you believe the training committee wants to hear. Trust that there is a match for you—the real you. Second, it is important to present yourself as a unique psychologist-in-training. Read each paragraph of your essay draft, and ask yourself, "Have I written anything in this section that couldn't also have been written by 75% of other applicants to this site?" If the answer is no, then you need some more "you" in that essay. Naturally, you do not want to differentiate yourself using a gimmick (a silly anecdote, story, or peculiar "overshare"), but you do want to ensure that your ideas reflect the unique person you are, given your unique training path to date.

It may be helpful to approach the essays with the following ideas in mind. For the past several years, you have been identified mostly as a student in a specific program as mentored by a specific advisor. You likely have introduced yourself to psychologists in the field with this information as markers of your professional identity. Your experiences in the field largely have been contained within the walls of your psychology department at your university.

This application process requires you to establish and convey a more specific identity that is unique to you. You are still the product of your program and advisor's mentorship, but this no longer is sufficient to describe the psychologist-in-training that you are now and the psychologist that you hope to be. Your path to doctoral study was unique; your reasons for attending your program and the choices you have made while engaged in it are part of your individual story. More important, the constellation of experiences you have accrued and the reflections you have had on these experiences throughout graduate school are unique to you and you alone. Why did you choose these specific practicum placements, and why did you select your specific thesis topics? What were your reactions to each of these experiences, and how did these reactions help shape your opinions about current issues in the field? What are your unique training goals, and how did you develop them? This is your story, and this is what you want to reflect in your essays (and interviews). This story differs from every other applicant's, and this is what makes you a unique candidate for a specific site.

You have 2,000 words with which to accomplish these objectives, divided among one very important cover letter and four specific essays. The story is a continuous one that starts with an "abstract" to your application that reviews the major themes and areas of fit (the cover letter), followed by a description of your experiences and goals

(Essay 1); elaborates through a discussion of your thoughts on a few important issues in our field today (e.g., theoretical conceptualization/orientation, client diversity) in Essays 2–3; and then focuses on your specific research interests in Essay 4.

A discussion of each specific essay is included below, followed by a discussion of the cover letter. We discuss the cover letter last because students typically work on this document after they have finished their initial four essays. We also have included some examples of actual essays used by applicants in recent years (with identifying information modified). With these applicants' permission, we have included, first, one example of a first draft, comments, and the corresponding final draft of an Essay 1, with additional final draft samples, to help you see the evolution of the writing process. The chapter then discusses and provides examples of final drafts of Essays 2 through 4, as well as a sample cover letter.

Note that the online APPI will allow you to write several different versions of your essays, and then append the appropriate versions to each specific application. For Essays 1–4, it may not be entirely necessary to construct different versions, if you have been consistent in your internship goals. However, if you find that you are applying to quite different types of sites (e.g., counseling centers vs. VA settings), then you may indeed want to craft modified versions of your essays for each type of site and must be sure to upload the appropriate version for each different type of site.

AUTOBIOGRAPHICAL STATEMENT, ESSAY 1 *Please provide an autobiographical statement. (There is no "correct" format for this question. Answer this question as if someone had asked you, "Tell me something about yourself." It is an opportunity for you to provide the internship site with some information about yourself. It is entirely up to you to decide what information you wish to provide along with the format in which to present it.)*

Essay 1 often is considered the most difficult essay because it also has the most ambiguous purpose. It is also not possible to write a full autobiography in 500 words, unless you seriously lack depth. Some sites prefer to get to know you as a person, including interests both inside and outside of psychology. The committee may wish to obtain some insight regarding your personality and background and perhaps catch a glimpse of the kind of person you would be during a social interaction. Other sites might be most interested in a professional autobiography, including a discussion of the factors that led to your decision to pursue a career in psychology and a brief review of your experiences, culminating in a discussion of your goals for internship training. Still other sites are interested in assessing how you decided to approach this essay, having no preconceived opinion of a type of essay that is preferable.

How do you know what the site wants to hear? Unfortunately, you will not know. Some anecdotal evidence suggests that many counseling centers or sites with psychodynamic training may prefer the personal approach, whereas research-oriented sites, or sites with a cognitive-behavioral orientation, might prefer a focus on your professional history. Ultimately, this is a decision that you will need to make on the basis of your own comfort level and disposition. Remember, you are not merely looking for a slot; you are looking for a good fit. If the autobiographical statement truly reflects your style, you are increasing the chances that you will find a true fit.

Still, this is a hard task. The following tips will help you get started with the autobiographical statement.

- *Tell a story.* In other words, describe yourself and your experience in a manner that has a beginning, a middle, and an end. You may wish to start with a depiction of the person you were before graduate school and end with the person you want to be after internship. You may also want to select one story out of your autobiography to highlight that has been particularly meaningful to you in your development as a psychologist.
- *State your goals.* Explain to the reader where your internship goals came from. Demonstrate to the committee that these are well-thought-out goals that were developed through a careful review of your past experiences and career objectives. You may even wish to discuss these goals with a supervisor for assistance. If your goals seem to be tacked on to the end of the essay with no explanation or foreshadowing, a cynical reviewer may think that you have disingenuously changed them for each site to "appear" to be a match.
- *Do not restate your CV.* Rather, "walk the reader through" it. What are the most important experiences on your CV? What are the themes that have emerged across all of your experiences? Is there something you are especially proud of that you would like to highlight? Don't talk about what you did but, rather, what you thought while doing it.
- *Talk about the future.* Internship sites know what they are good at and where their interns have gone following training. Giving them a sense of where you may want to go will help the committee to know whether they can provide you with the experiences you need. Although you may not need to have a clear idea of your future plans (most do not at this stage), you can probably rule in or out at least two or three options.

Recall that Essay 1, if structured properly, could serve as an organizing theme for the entire set of essays. Hence, you should embed statements about your approach to cases, your experience with diversity, your research goals, and your fit with the site. By constructing the first essay in this manner, your set of essays is more likely to read as a detailed description of you as a professional rather than as a series of fragmented details.

Below is an example of a first draft of an autobiographical statement, followed by comments that are common for many students as they write this statement.

Essay 1, First Draft

I did not always want to be a psychologist. Actually, it was not until the second semester of my junior year that I found the profession. There was not some big incident or exciting story behind my changing from economics to psychology. In fact, my professional identity has continued to slowly evolve from that initial switch, and now, I could not imagine another career that would be better suited to me. Every step in the evolution has added an important perspective or life goal, and I feel fortunate to have been able to pursue this path.

The allure of working with children first drew my attention to psychology as a career. Working as a child clinician resonated with my sense of fun and imagination. When I started doing clinical work with children, I also loved having to always think on my feet and being drawn into their worlds. I found it challenging to think about how to help a 7-year-old change his or her behavior, thoughts, or feelings, but also how different it would be to help a 15-year-old. I take pleasure in knowing that every time I walk into a room with kids, anything can happen. In my clinical work, I also find inspiration for research and how to examine psychopathology. Moreover, the aspects of my personality that fit child clinical work (sense of fun, curiosity, energetic, and imagination) also help me be a better researcher and teacher.

Although I had participated in research at college, it was not until I developed my own research questions and tested them that I began to see research as a part of my professional identity. I became involved in an applied developmental research laboratory working with Latino immigrants. Taking part in both design and data collection of an intervention study, I began to see how clinical work and research both inform one another. At this time, my own research questions began to surface, and as I watched parents, children, and teachers interacting, I became interested in the interpersonal aspects of maladaptive behavior.

Teaching was the last aspect of the profession to which I was exposed, but one that I find immensely satisfying. Since starting graduate school, I have taught my own course, mentored students on their own research projects, and supervised students doing clinical work. In all of these teaching endeavors, I have hoped to instill an appreciation for curiosity, passion, knowledge, and cultural differences. Moreover, like my clinical work, teaching also provides me with continued energy for my own research.

My current professional path is as a matter of fact not that different from my initial career goal. By first grade I wanted to become a doctor and join the Peace Corps so that I could provide medical services to those with no access. What drew me to that profession at such a young age is probably what drives my current professional goals to become a clinical psychology professor researching clinical interventions in underserved populations, specifically Latinos. My compassion and dedication to helping the underserved have not wavered, and I do not need to go to a developing nation. Fewer than 1% of psychologists are Latinos, and as a professor I will be able to be a model for other minority students, challenge and teach undergraduates be cognizant of cultural issues, and train future clinicians in cultural competence. At each step of my path, whether it be clinical work, research, or teaching, I have increased my skills and knowledge. I look forward to continue evolving on internship, where I hope to get added training.

Essay 1, Comments

This is a well-written essay that effectively achieves several of the objectives outlined above. Indeed, as a first draft, this student has done a terrific job in many respects. First, the essay tells a compelling story with a beginning, middle, and end. It is clear how this student's interests have evolved over time, and a clear set of career goals has been articulated. Second, the essay is written in a knowledgeable yet personal voice.

There are several ways in which this essay could be improved. First, although the story of the applicant's decision to enter graduate school is compelling and interesting, the text regarding the decision to enter doctoral studies dominates about two thirds of the essay. This is common among first drafts; they often sound a lot like the essay that was used when applying to graduate school, rather than an essay that is focused on internship. Given that all applicants at this stage have already made the decision to pursue a graduate career, and all have already been in graduate training, this information is not as useful in helping to describe what kind of psychologist-in-training the applicant is now. It may be more helpful to discuss the graduate experiences that have shaped this applicant's internship goals.

It is also common, in autobiographical essay first drafts, for internship goals not to have been clearly articulated. Rather, the strongest message that is conveyed in this draft is that the applicant is enthusiastic about clinical child psychology. This is a wonderful sentiment to convey; however, it may not adequately distinguish the applicant from others. From the perspective of an internship selection committee, it is difficult to determine whether this student will thrive at a specific site and whether the site is a good fit. It would be helpful to understand what kind of psychologist-in-training this applicant has become, and what principles guide this applicant's decisions.

Last, this essay is overly modest. This applicant has achieved a great deal while in graduate school, but those achievements have not been adequately reflected in the essay.

Essay 1, Final Draft

Clinical work first drew me into the profession of psychology. When I started doing clinical work with children, I enjoyed the challenge of helping children understand their emotional worlds and change through the use of cognitive-behavioral techniques. Yet, I realized that integrating other theoretical perspectives, such as developmental approaches, significantly improved therapeutic responses. Nevertheless, because the majority of interventions did not address issues of diversity, I found myself having to adapt treatments to fit the cultural contexts of my clients. This knowledge led me to wonder how treatments might better address issues of culture, and I began to see the development of these manuals as part of my future career. Moreover, as one of the few Spanish-speaking therapists in my community, I continually received referrals for Latino clients, and I realized that Latinos have limited access to culturally competent mental health services. This not only motivated me to work in various clinical settings where I was able to apply my linguistic and cultural knowledge but also refined my career goal to the development of treatments tailored for the Latino community.

Although I had thought of myself primarily as a clinician in the past, research is now central to my career goals. Through clinical work, I started to develop research questions concerning the interpersonal antecedents of maladaptive behavior. My master's thesis examined the differential prediction of perceived peer rejection and victimization on adolescent psychological outcomes. After completing my master's, I received a grant to pursue friendship processes associated with adolescent depression. I am especially interested in understanding the quantification of dyadic processes and how children and adolescents internalize and cope with interpersonal distress. Given the interpersonal focus of various cultural groups, I see this research in line with the development of culturally tailored interventions for children, adolescents, and families.

In addition to my clinical and research interests, my experiences teaching and supervising have led me to hope that one day I will pursue a career as a professor in a university setting. In my 4th year, I became the advanced student graduate supervisor for our department's child practicum. Providing supervision not only enhanced my own clinical and case conceptualization skills but also afforded me the opportunity to teach others how to think clinically. I greatly enjoyed being able to challenge students and shape how they understood clinical phenomena and interventions. For example, in the application of a parenting manual, one of the students failed to recognize clinical moments that might have led the parents to a deeper understanding of their parenting. Instead, the student mechanically led the parents through the prescribed tasks. In the use of clinical manuals, I find it is more important to be true to the theoretical mechanisms of change than to the specific tasks. I helped her notice these "clinical windows" and understand how the manual conceptualized change processes, leading her to be able to use these opportunities to achieve change.

Throughout graduate school, I have taken advantage of opportunities to grow professionally, and I hope to continue to do so during internship. I look forward to internship training that will provide me with (a) additional multicultural training with Latino populations; (b) continued exposure to a variety of theoretical orientations; and (c) an opportunity to learn evidence-based treatments for adolescent depression. I believe these goals are essential to my career objectives, and I am excited that such experiences appear to be available at your training site.

More Sample Essay 1 Responses

Please note: All biographical and other identifying information has been removed from the sample essays shown here. Remember, these additional examples are not necessarily ideal or flawless, but they represent the types of essays that former applicants have submitted.

Sample Essay 1A. I approached psychology very seriously as an undergraduate student, and I arrived to the University of X eager to begin my training as a clinical psychologist. I did not anticipate, however, just how out of place I would initially feel. It had not occurred to me that being the youngest of my cohort, the sole individual from the Deep South, and the one student who was the first in their family to attend college would set me apart. For the first time in my life, I questioned whether I was prepared for the endeavors before me. I did not dress like my classmates, come from a comparable background, or even use a similar vocabulary. I imagined that these differences surely would create a problem. What I found, in contrast, is that my differences contribute to my strengths as a clinical psychologist. My background and the individuality it helped to shape remain important influences and have allowed me to retain my*self* as a tool in the therapy room.

The science *and* art of clinical psychology are what attracted me to the field. The complexity involved in "getting it right" and balancing the two aspects of clinical practice is a never-ending pursuit that maintains my excitement for this work. My clinical training has been firmly grounded in cognitive behavior theory and developmental theory, and I am committed to the integration of science and practice. In addition, I believe that evidence-based conceptualization and treatment are informed optimally by flexible thinking that is based on the integration of relevant theoretical perspectives. Thus, augmenting my training with an increased understanding of other theoretical orientations is necessary to strengthen my identity and subsequent practice as a clinical psychologist. Indeed, such additional training is a primary goal of my internship year.

My clinical interests evolved from my undergraduate research experiences with delinquent youth. I realized that these children had not been troubled since birth, and I wanted to understand how some youth succumb to risk while others remain resilient. I also became keenly aware that the services these youth received typically were insufficient, and I wondered about the most effective ways to treat children and adolescents. Thus, my research naturally informed my clinical interests and thinking. Since then, I have been particularly invested in working with underserved and at-risk populations, with a specific interest in how contextual factors may exacerbate or ameliorate their adjustment. To this end, I have sought training experiences with children and adults from diverse racial, ethnic, and socioeconomic backgrounds. Also, I have worked to increase my familiarity with the multiple sources that can potentially serve as points of intervention, including various treatment modalities, therapeutic settings, and consultation sources. This breadth of experience has been invaluable in informing my professional growth.

I view my clinical internship as a crucial step in my professional development, and my goal is to build on the foundation of my training thus far. Thus, I am interested in continued work with underserved populations, particularly youth and their families. I envision refining and expanding upon my skills in assessment and intervention via training that is informed by a range of theoretical orientations and exposure to diverse client populations.

Sample Essay 1B. As I ponder my life thus far, a quotation by William Hazlitt (1778) comes to mind: "A strong passion . . . will insure success, for the desire of the end will point out the means." *Ambition, passion, service, motivation,* and *persistence* are words that have dominated my life's work and created my life's path. These sustaining qualities have been both influenced and maintained by significant individuals and by experiences throughout the years.

I am the oldest of a family of four children raised in a small poor rural town. Heavily influenced by a Russian Judaic background and Native American spirituality, our family struggled to fit into the social mold. Despite the obstacles that surrounded my childhood years, my parents were supportive and encouraged me to strive to reach my full potential. My family's constant belief that you can create your destiny, as well as their belief in my talents and ability to contribute to the healing profession, planted the first seeds of motivation and passion for service.

Growing up in a family of healers, I quickly discovered the value of providing assistance to those in need. Thus, when I was in sixth grade I made the decision to pursue a career as a psychologist. In college, my first experience in the field was working with emotionally disturbed and sexually abused young women. In addition, it was at this time that a close friend was assaulted. I saw clearly for the first time the power of a psychologist's work, and my commitment to women's issues, trauma recovery, and my career path was solidified. In continued pursuit of my passion and ambition for service, I sought a master's degree. It was during my master's program that fervor for research and for the substance use field developed. However, this program also created a thirst for more knowledge and experience. Thus, I enrolled in a doctoral program in counseling psychology.

I have developed my skills, interests, and identity as a mental health professional through a variety of mentoring relationships and educational and training experiences.

These relationships and experiences have helped me gather the strength and fortitude to trust myself and to utilize my strengths. They have also helped maintain my commitment, dedication, and passion for psychology. In addition, my relationships and experiences have also taught me the necessity in balancing my career aspirations with a personal life. To rejuvenate, I enjoy time with my animals, hiking, meditating, or reading a favorite philosopher. Additionally, I love to travel, to dance, and to participate in a variety of advocacy groups.

Hence, not only have my passion and commitment to my work been unwavering, they have been the impetus for a variety of meaningful professional and personal experiences. Thus far, I feel proud of where my passion and dedication have brought me and feel excited about where they might take me. I look forward to the prospect of having them bring the opportunity to personally introduce myself to you.

Sample Essay 1C. I certainly cannot say that I expected to become a clinical psychologist from an early age. Indeed, growing up in a hard-working family in [city, state], where my father and older brothers are mechanics, a career in psychology was well off my anticipated path. However, I was introduced to clinical psychology as a high school senior and was immediately fascinated by the models I learned about that explained different facets of human behavior. These models greatly facilitated my understanding of the functions, orderliness, and predictability of many behaviors, and the applications appeared endless. More recently, I have learned to use clinical psychology not only as a means to understand the actions of others, but more importantly, as a vehicle for helping to improve people's functioning and mental health, which I think is really the most valuable thing one has.

The significance of accurately evaluating and treating psychopathology became particularly clear to me during a college internship in a locked psychiatric unit for violent inpatients during a semester abroad. This unique experience confirmed my interest in clinical work but also triggered a whole set of questions in my mind that remain at the center of my clinical and research interests: Why do some people repeatedly engage in aggressive behaviors, while others are compelled to hurt themselves? Why are some virtually paralyzed by anxiety and depression? How can we change the behaviors of those who want help? What about those who do not? After consulting my supervisors and visiting the library, I was intrigued and motivated to learn that the answers to such crucial questions remain, to a large extent, unknown.

Over the next several years, I deliberately sought out a wide range of clinical and research positions in the mental health field that approached the understanding and treatment of these problems from a number of different perspectives. Through each of these unique experiences, I consistently realized the value and importance of using systematic observation and evaluation as a means of studying these phenomena and developing effective treatments. Consequently, I chose to attend the doctoral program at X University because of its strong commitment to the scientist–practitioner training model. This training has taught me not only to be a consumer of clinical research but also to use scientific methods to continually evaluate the treatments I provide and to actively contribute to the larger scientific and clinical community. For instance, I have completed several clinically relevant studies on the development and treatment of aggression, anxiety, and suicidal behaviors. Moreover, my National Institute of Mental Health (NIMH)–funded dissertation research is focused on evaluating the effectiveness of a therapy preparation component, which I developed based on recent research conducted at our clinic, to increase participation and therapeutic change in child therapy. Such an interaction between science and practice is what continues to excite me about this work and is a consistent theme in my approach to clinical and research activities.

I look forward to internship as a valuable opportunity to continue to obtain the best training experience possible in order to strengthen the foundation on which I will build my career as a clinician, researcher, and teacher. I am strongly interested in the internship program at [Your Site] because it offers the most logical continuation of my scientist–practitioner training, as well as exciting opportunities to expand on my knowledge of evidenced-based treatments and to continue to apply these interventions to a wide variety of clients (children, adolescents, and adults) in diverse settings (outpatient and inpatient). I hope I will have the opportunity to receive this training at [Your Site] and to be as much of a benefit to the internship program as I know it will be to me.

THEORETICAL ORIENTATION, ESSAY 2

Please describe your theoretical orientation and how this influences your approach to case conceptualization and intervention. You may use de-identified case material to illustrate your points if you choose.

Essays 2 and 3 often are regarded as exercises in which one feels pulled to give the "right" answer. In other words, these essays sometimes seem to be academic or evaluative, and you may feel motivated to demonstrate your knowledge from coursework. However, this is not an optimal approach. Again, consider how to make yourself a unique applicant and help the reader think of you as someone the reader would be excited to work with in supervision. For example, defining cognitive behavior therapy in Essay 2 is of no help to those who read the essays. They understand the basic tenets of all the major theoretical orientations and do not need brief lessons in them or a demonstration that you know them. Although it is important to demonstrate knowledge of the field and of psychological theory and practice in these essays, we suggest that it is more important to discuss your personal opinions, beliefs, and practices in the essay. It is OK to take a stand and discuss your beliefs. Remember, you are applying for a training position, and your openness to learning, growing, and further developing your theoretical orientation is important.

Essay 2 is used to help you explain the type of training models you were exposed to in your graduate program and the type of training you would like to receive on internship. You may wish to convey past experiences by using a case example, or not. You should most certainly discuss future training in an explicit way. If you have chosen a particular site because of its theoretical orientation, then say so! And—very important— integrate some statements regarding your goals and discuss the manner in which your case conceptualization skills will both fit the site and be further cultivated by the training experiences that the site has to offer. You don't need a different Essay 2 for every site, but if you picked your sites with consistent goals in mind, a broad statement about what kind of training/supervision you are looking for during internship will work for all of your sites.

You may use some of these questions to help you write this essay.

- How do you approach cases theoretically? Be clear about your theoretical orientation to your clinical work. Why do you have this orientation, and what more would you like to learn?

- What is your approach to assessment? Do you consider differential diagnoses? Do you explore themes in the pattern of your client's relationships or the style in which these experiences are discussed by the client? Were there early experiences that were pivotal in shaping your assessment approach?
- How do you proceed with treatment? Do you measure relevant outcomes as you progress? Do you establish treatment goals? How do you know when treatment is over? What are your beliefs about treatment orientations, and how do you think the future of field will deal with disparate orientations?
- What are your strengths and weaknesses in case conceptualization? Yes, it is OK to discuss weaknesses (i.e., areas for which you would like to receive additional training). Internship is a training experience, and you should explain how you would like to be trained.

Try to carry the same themes you discussed in your autobiographic essay into Essay 2. This is important to help you demonstrate and reiterate your training goals.

Sample Responses for Essay 2

Sample Essay 2A. My approach to case conceptualization and treatment is an integrative process heavily influenced by four main factors: (a) the developmental psychopathology perspective that has enriched my understanding of how normal and abnormal functioning develops across the life span, (b) the cognitive-behavioral framework within which I have been predominantly trained, (c) my strong commitment to the integration of science and practice, and (d) my pursuit of breadth and depth in understanding the clients with whom I work.

When a client has been referred for treatment, my initial focus is on comprehensively assessing who this person is and how she developed the presenting problems. In doing so, the developmental psychopathology perspective as well as Bronfenbrenner's bioecological model have taught me to consider the multiple systems that may be contributing to the client's primary concerns. This is particularly important when working with a child or adolescent and includes consideration of her particular point in development. Thus, assessment focuses on individual characteristics (e.g., thinking and behavioral patterns); the family system, peers, and other important social influences; and the broader cultural community within which the client is embedded. My approach also emphasizes the interdependence of these multiple levels, leading to consideration of how my client impacts and contributes to her environment. This recognition of bidirectionality further helps me understand my client's unique strengths and weaknesses as they apply to questions of minimizing risk and enhancing resiliency, and this assessment directly impacts my treatment plan.

After a rich conceptualization has been developed during the initial assessment phase, I begin constructing a plan for intervention. Given my allegiance to the integration of science and practice in my clinical work, the initial treatment plan often involves consulting the relevant research literatures as needed. Additionally, I often consult evidence-based manuals that have demonstrated effectiveness with populations having backgrounds and circumstances similar to my client's. Given that the cognitive-behavioral framework has been studied, and more readily applied, to the treatment of psychopathology than any other approach, cognitive behavior therapy often provides the foundation for building an effective treatment strategy. Furthermore, given my emphasis on the multiple systems involved in development and change, I also carefully consider how to incorporate relevant systemic factors, whether directly or indirectly in the therapeutic process.

My view of psychotherapy is that the process is an ever-evolving one that involves ongoing assessment and feedback from the client in order to maximize treatment gains. This continual process often leads to consideration of how other theoretical perspectives can augment my conceptualization and thinking, and I have found it extremely beneficial to broaden the scope of my theoretical orientation in order to gain greater depth in understanding my clients. Thus, dynamic and interpersonal theories have bolstered my understanding of how psychopathology develops and manifests across the life course, as well as how the therapeutic process itself can be influenced by a person's history. The field of psychopharmacology has augmented my understanding of the interplay between biology and psychology. Multicultural theories have enhanced my awareness and sensitivity to some of the more subtle ways in which culture and identity can impact a client. I view these, as well as other relevant perspectives, as essential tools in adding to the breadth and depth necessary in order to optimally understand and treat clients with the care, respect, and expertise they deserve. Thus, my goal for the internship year is to continue refining and expanding upon my conceptualization and treatment skills by gaining increased exposure, understanding, and comfort with multiple theoretical perspectives.

Sample Essay 2B. Innate empathy, genuine concern, and compassion are personal attributes that I bring to my role as a trainee. These characteristics have been the foundation on which my clinical strengths have emerged and continue to develop. I am able to aptly identify client strengths and resiliencies that can be used as anchoring points for productive client change, leaving clients with a sense of empowerment and dignity in situations that may appear hopeless, stressful, overwhelming, or defeating. I seek to establish a cooperative environment that allows for the exchange of ideas and expertise in the therapy process. I used diagnosis as a mechanism for client change and insight.

Rather than offering a diagnosis as the answer to the client's problem situation, I prefer to use diagnosis as a springboard for generative therapeutic conversation. This approach is consistent with my theoretical orientation.

Postmodern assumptions that include social constructivism and narrative approaches to therapy inform the way I think about and talk with clients. I organize my thinking through the metaphors of narration (or storytelling) and social construction. I conceptualize problems as being separate from the person experiencing the difficulties. Many problems are stories that clients construct through social interaction. These socially constructed realities provide the beliefs, practices, words, and experiences from which clients create their life stories and constitute themselves. The meanings that clients attribute to the events and experiences in their lives create their reality. Because meaning is created through individuals in conversation, new meaning and a new reality can be introduced by changing the stories clients tell themselves. Every client has his or her own version of truth with its own inherent logic. Clients interpret their experiences based upon their version of truth, and these realities, or truths, can be organized, maintained, or changed through modifying the types of conversations to which clients are engaged in or exposed.

Similarly, assessment can be useful in offering one possible life story for clients to accept, reject, or change. Given the dynamic nature of assessments, these tools can help provide direction for the client and therapist in determining which aspects of the client's story they wish to retain and which they would like to change. From a consultative perspective, helping clients create alternate meanings for symptoms creates opportunities for change and intervention rather than restricting options. For me, good clinical interviews determine the appropriate diagnostic tests to administer and the subsequent use of those tests in understanding and treating the client's presenting problems. I do not use any predetermined set of tests for every client I see, as the nature of the client's problems and needs will dictate the tests and interventions used.

Sample Essay 2C. My approach to case conceptualization, evaluation, and treatment planning is primarily behavioral and cognitive-behavioral in nature and is strongly influenced by the principles of learning (e.g., operant and classical conditioning paradigms). Although learning theory is most often associated with behavioral and cognitive-behavioral treatments, the basic elements of this theoretical framework are pervasive in cognitive, psychodynamic, humanistic, and other treatment approaches, strengthening the appeal and the applicability of this approach.

The first, and perhaps most important, step in my application of this approach to a clinical case is the use of comprehensive, reliable, and valid assessments that draw on multiple methods and informants and that continue to test, inform, and guide the case conceptualization and intervention plan throughout treatment. My next step is the collaborative development of a clear and specific list of presenting problems and an evaluation of the clinical severity and impairment associated with each problem. At the center of my case conceptualization is a generation of hypotheses about the function of each problem behavior, including an analysis of factors that may be causing or maintaining these problems (e.g., antecedents and consequences of each behavior) and about the interrelation of the presenting problems.

My treatment plan follows directly from my primary case conceptualization. On the most basic level, whatever maladaptive learning has occurred must be "unlearned" (e.g., an association between a feared object and anxiety is weakened via exposure) and whatever adaptive learning has not occurred must be learned (e.g., prosocial behavior is increased when followed by positive reinforcement). As assessment and treatment are inseparable elements from my perspective, the continuous evaluation of the target problems is a critical component of my approach. The information provided by frequent and continued assessments is used to test the effectiveness of the intervention and to modify my conceptualization and treatment plan as necessary. In addition, my treatment plan incorporates evidence-based treatment techniques or treatment packages when available and is based directly on the principles of learning whenever possible.

I particularly enjoy working from a learning perspective because this approach is straightforward, flexible, parsimonious, widely applicable, and evidence based. I look forward to receiving additional training in the use of evidence-based evaluation and treatment procedures during internship. Indeed, I am uniquely interested in the internship program at [site] because of the attention given to such approaches in didactic instruction, clinical training, and case supervision, as well as the rich opportunities to interact with clinicians and supervisors working from a wide range of case conceptualization approaches to which I have had less exposure (such as psychodynamic and interpersonal approaches), as these are my main goals for the internship year. Moreover, the application of such approaches to the treatment of impulsive, anxious, and depressed children and adolescents, such as that offered in the [Site Center] rotations at the Institute for the Study of Psychological Service and the Anxiety and Mood Disorders Service, are a direct match with my previous training and current interests, and I look forward to the chance to learn more about these opportunities.

DIVERSITY
EXPERIENCE,
ESSAY 3

Please describe your experience and training in work with diverse populations. Your discussion should display explicitly the manner in which multicultural/diversity issues influence your clinical practice and case conceptualization.

You likely have discussed the importance of diversity and cultural competence in your classes, and you likely recognize that you can overlay a cultural framework onto virtually every activity you engage in as a psychologist. This essay gives you an opportunity to discuss your thoughts and experiences regarding issues of diversity in greater detail.

An essay summarizing all of your clients who are demographically different from you may not be the best use of this essay. Much of this information could be gleaned from your AAPI and CV, and this approach does not reflect your thinking and your development as a psychologist-in-training.

Some applicants tell a story of a particular experience with a client in which they had a significant insight regarding the importance of cultural competence that forever changed their approach to clinical work. This may yield a more useful and interesting essay, but keep in mind that this approach is quite common and does not often differentiate applicants.

In fact, the vast majority of essays read something like this:

> I believe multiculturalism is important. Indeed, I have worked with many clients who are demographically different from myself, including a, b, c, d, e, and even f. Here is a case example: I once had a client who was different than me on variable X. They said one thing, I thought another. Then, I realized that I had to consider variable X. I had an epiphany! Once we talked about variable X, it changed my conceptualization on this case and we all lived happily ever after. I want to continue to think about diversity training on internship.

If this is what your first draft sounds like, please start again.

An approach to this essay that most certainly will differentiate your application is to discuss something that is unique to you—that is, your beliefs, your thoughts, and your ideas. In addition to the types of messages conveyed above (i.e., discussing past experiences or pivotal moments), you also can use this essay to discuss your thoughts regarding what you believe to be the future needs in the field, how you believe your training would benefit from specific types of experiences, and what specific competencies you feel you have developed regarding cultural competence. How could, should, or would you incorporate these ideas into clinical practice and research? Similarly, as you increasingly have become a more culturally competent individual who is sensitive to the range of diversity issues, what has surprised you the most about what you have learned about yourself in this process? What are you particularly proud of, or what are some areas that have been a struggle for you?

Consider addressing the following questions when planning your essay.

- What does diversity mean to you?
- What situation did you experience when you recognized that diversity was important to consider? Remember, diversity can refer to demographic, geographic, or ideological heterogeneity among your past clients.
- Have your experiences led you to develop specific (primary or supplemental) training goals related to diversity?
- How do these goals match the opportunities offered at this training site? What are your multicultural counseling competencies? What are your weaknesses in this area?

Sample Responses for Essay 3

Sample Essay 3A. Embracing a multicultural perspective is an integral component of every case conceptualization and treatment plan. This has been salient particularly in my work with underserved populations, but it is equally relevant to every individual because we all develop within a cultural context. Thus, viewing clients through a cultural lens allows for greater awareness of the multitude of risk and protective factors that may be contributing to their clinical presentations. This does not mean that aspects of culture always play a primary role in explaining the development of psychopathology. However, a critical part of all assessments is careful consideration of the relevant contextual factors that may have important implications for treatment. Some features of a client's cultural context are more salient than others and have clear links with a person's adjustment, such as how an individual's race may lead to experiences with discrimination. Equally important, however, is consideration of the more subtle ways in which a person's culture may affect functioning, such as how a person's cultural upbringing may inform the most effective therapeutic modality or how a person's gender or race may affect his symptom presentation.

Sensitivity to the cultural factors influencing an individual's circumstances is not only beneficial to the therapist, it can have a remarkable impact on clients as well. For instance, in treating a lesbian couple who presented with relationship dissatisfaction, one salient issue addressed in therapy was how each partner's identity with regard to gay culture differed substantially from the other, and this resulted in miscommunications that exacerbated hostility and resentment between them. Explicit discussion of each partner's frame of reference gave the other insight into her partner's motivations that she had no awareness of prior to therapy. This led to increased empathy and understanding between them, which served to enhance the overall quality of their relationship.

Although I believe that it is essential to situate each client within a multicultural framework, I also think that it is extremely important to recognize that the guiding principles of a multicultural model should not be used as a means for stereotyping and categorizing in order to simplify a client's unique development and presentation. Thus, it is essential to acknowledge differences but not let that unduly influence case conceptualization and interpretation. Rather, a multicultural framework should allow for an enriched understanding of the complexity of a client's motives, strengths, and vulnerabilities. Intragroup variations are a critical component of such a framework.

I have a strong commitment to issues of diversity, and I view related education and training as an integral component of my work. I have sought experiences with diverse clinical populations, and I also have chosen to focus my independent research projects on the adjustment of African American youth from single-mother homes. In addition, I have been actively involved in my program's diversity committee, diversity-related workshops, and minority-focused seminars. In my opinion, multicultural training is not something that can be learned in a single course or in working with a single client. Rather, it is an ever-evolving process that continues throughout professional development. Moreover, part of the learning experience has been in recognizing the cultural context within which I have developed so that I can continue to develop a greater awareness of my own biases and how they influence the ways in which I interpret and respond to clients. Thus, continued exposure to diverse client populations is one of my primary objectives for internship.

Sample Essay 3B. I believe it is essential—particularly as an individual aspiring to a career of service to the distressed—to remain sensitive, always, to multicultural issues. As a member of several categories of the majority culture who has benefited from a lifetime of relative privilege, visible and invisible, there was a time when I was far more naïve regarding this responsibility. Several life experiences, clinical contacts, and formal trainings have proven indelible and transformative to me in the trajectory toward multicultural competence in my clinical practice. One stands out. Over the summer before applying to graduate school, I lived in Arusha, Tanzania, and worked at an orphanage and school for children. As one of a small handful of "mzungu" or White people living among a homogenous Black population, I had never felt so constantly and intensely scrutinized by the people around me for my outward appearance. When I walked to work every morning, a growing chorus of children would trail, shouting, "Mzungu! Mzungu!" I had never fully felt the pervasive and exhausting experience of stereotype threat until, on several occasions, good friends asked me questions like, "As a White person, what do you think about . . . ?" or "What does it feel like to be White?" This experience and a few invaluable others have provided me with rare opportunities to travel as a "tourist" within a dramatically different cultural identity. Although it seems obvious that one's cultural characteristics are most visible against a starkly contrasted majority culture's, it is difficult to know how profoundly this can be felt unless one experiences it.

This kind of experience has helped shape and give depth to my clinical work with diverse populations. Two principles most prominently underlie my current approach to multiculturally informed practice. First, I believe that multiculturalism must be defined as an almost infinitely broad construct. In some senses there are aspects of every individual's cultural background and identity that may distinguish him or her even from immediate family members. (For example, as the youngest and only male child in a family of six I need no reminders of how differently my sisters and I have conceptualized our upbringing.) In essence, everyone has a unique story. Of course, individuals who would seem to have obvious differences in their evident culture—across such categories as gender, sexual identity/orientation, ethnicity, or socioeconomic status—may share far more similarities than differences. An important lesson for my clinical practice is the realization that it is never safe to make assumptions, either about the background experiences or cultural identities of the individual before me or about the ways in which each individual's unique strengths and vulnerabilities may (or may not) be shaped by culture.

Logically extending this point relates to the second principle guiding my clinical practice. The concept of "multicultural competence" is far from an enlightened state at which one aspires to arrive. Rather, it is an attitude and orientation to clinical work. It is not enough, for example, for a competent practitioner to educate him- or herself about diverse populations and phenomena within them. (In fact, the use of such knowledge derived from groups must be used cautiously so as not to obscure potentially more important individual differences.) True competence entails a lifelong process of "listening" carefully and developing greater awareness, both of the client's background and of one's own cultural schema and biases.

Continuing my own development as a multiculturally competent clinician is one of my major goals for internship. It is my hope that this year will present opportunities for more focused and varied exposure to clients with diverse backgrounds and identities across developmental stages. An internship within an urban medical center, medical school, or consortium would be the ideal setting to accomplish this goal.

Sample Essay 3C. I am fortunate to have had a wealth of clinical and training experiences with diverse populations up to this point in my career, and I look forward to building on these experiences during internship. At X University, diversity training is an integral part of the course curriculum and clinical training. For instance, we have a weekly, semester-long seminar series focusing on clinical research relevant to ethnic and cultural diversity presented by eminent researchers from around the country. In addition, issues of socioeconomic, ethnic, and cultural diversity have been explicitly addressed in each of my clinical practica at X University, through which I evaluated and treated a diverse client population from the [City, State, Area]. Also, as an active member of my department's diversity committee, I am helping to develop methods of diversifying our own graduate student population and training experience.

The clinical experiences I had before graduate school also provided the opportunity to work with unique and diverse populations. For instance, in Europe, I worked at a psychiatric hospital that served a large, urban catchment area and that had a violent, severely ill, and socioculturally diverse population. In X City, my experiences ranged from working for a corporate managed health care organization serving professional clientele to working as an intake clinician at X Outpatient Service, a homeless shelter for an under-21 population consisting primarily of low-income minority adolescents. These experiences with truly diverse populations have prepared me well for future work in a range of clinical settings.

As a result of my training and clinical experiences, issues of ethnic, cultural, and socioeconomic diversity influence my case conceptualization, assessment, and treatment procedures in several ways. First, I routinely evaluate whether (and how) a client or family's cultural beliefs influence his or her view of the presenting problems. For example, ethnic and cultural differences in parenting style (e.g., permissiveness vs. strictness) have been well documented and can often influence a parent's perception of his or her child's behavior problems. Second, I similarly evaluate whether a client or family's cultural beliefs influence their view of psychotherapy in general or the specific treatment plan in particular. For instance, some of my research has demonstrated that African American and Latino families tend to view psychotherapy as less credible than do European American families and that this view may lead to decreased participation in treatment. Third, I evaluate whether a client or family's cultural beliefs influence the method of treatment delivery. For instance, I recently worked with a family from the Dominican Republic in which the success of the intervention was greatly facilitated by actively involving the father in treatment planning and implementation, as he was the head of the household and yielded a strong influence over the rules of the house and the disciplinary practices with the children. I believe that a failure to recognize this cultural dynamic could have led to a lack of treatment adherence or attrition from treatment altogether.

I believe it is essential for my development as a clinician and researcher that I continue to receive training and experiences in the treatment of diverse populations. Indeed, this diversity is one of the many things I enjoy about [City, State] and is one of the reasons I am enthusiastic about the possibility of participating in the internship program at [Site].

RESEARCH EXPERIENCE, ESSAY 4

Please describe your research experience and interests.

This essay may not seem applicable to all. Some applicants have already decided that their dissertation will be their last involvement in research activities. Others hope to gain substantial research experience on internship. Either way, you had major research milestones while in graduate school, so everyone should be able to write a good version of this essay that demonstrates his or her understanding of psychological theory, an empiricist approach, and an ability to translate hypotheses and findings into clinical implications.

You should approach this essay by discussing your research *program*. Start with a few statements regarding your philosophy about how human behavior and/or psychopathology "works." An overarching statement about your philosophy, interests, or beliefs will differentiate this statement from a mere list of your research projects in graduate school. In the paragraphs that follow, you will want to discuss each of your past graduate-level research experiences; the themes of your research program; your dissertation, including its (current and expected) completion status; and your interests regarding research training before and after internship. You also may wish to discuss how these research experiences have informed your clinical work. Provide a specific example or perhaps discuss a theory with clinical application.

You do not want this essay to sound as though you are applying for a research assistant position. A detailed list of your responsibilities (e.g., "I conducted 100 structured interviews!") is not as valuable as a discussion of your interests, the findings in your research, and their clinical implications.

Sample Responses for Essay 4

Sample Essay 4A. My program of research has evolved from my interest in the frameworks articulated by the developmental psychopathology perspective and Bronfenbrenner's bioecological model. Thus, I have collaborated on a number of projects that include consideration of the multiple dynamic systems that influence child development, including individual, family, and broader environmental factors. Moreover, I particularly am interested in understanding the development and treatment of internalizing behaviors in at-risk youth from understudied populations. Both my master's and dissertation projects focused on the ways in which neighborhood context influences the association between self-regulation difficulties and depression in African American youth.

Findings from my master's thesis revealed that disadvantaged neighborhoods exacerbated the relation between early maltreatment difficulties and depression in girls. Thus, in an effort to extend this preliminary investigation, my dissertation (to be completed prior to internship) further examines this association by including both objectively and subjectively defined indicators of neighborhood, as well as further examination of gender differences. Accordingly, my dissertation aims to address how variations in neighborhood assessment similarly or differently moderate the link between self-regulation difficulties and depression. Research such as this is necessary to identify the ways in which individual and environmental systems may interact to exacerbate, or alternatively, ameliorate a child's risk for psychopathology. My dissertation therefore will provide important clinical implications for African American youth, their families, and their communities. My hope is that this research will enhance the implementation of successful intervention efforts, as well as aid in the accurate identification of subgroups most in need of our treatment programs.

In addition to my independent research endeavors, I have collaborated with my advisor on a number of papers and presentations that broadly focus on the family as a context for studying both parental and child adjustment (please see my CV). For over a year, I also have served as the project coordinator of a grant-funded, community-based study examining the role of extended family members in the psychosocial adjustment of African American youth. I have been fortunate to be involved in virtually every aspect of the project, and my primary responsibilities include recruiting families, training and managing staff, and conducting the interviews. My integral involvement has been an invaluable learning experience and has provided an excellent model for how to design, implement, and execute a successful community-based research program.

I believe that sound clinical practice must be informed by research that addresses questions of how and why. Similarly, rich clinical experiences are the mechanisms through which meaningful research is fostered. Ultimately, I am interested in producing research that aids in the development of theoretically derived, culturally sensitive, multisystemic prevention and intervention programs. Accordingly, my hope for the internship year is that I will gain exposure to clinical experiences that will expand my knowledge base, refine my hypotheses, and incite questions that lead to further exploration of the multiple interdependent contexts within which youth develop.

Sample Essay 4B. As someone who embraces the scientist–practitioner model, my clinical interests and research interests are complementary. I have sought clinical training and a degree specialty in dual diagnosis, with trauma and substance use being the main foci. In addition, I have conducted research on, among other things, correlates of substance use and trauma, motivation and substance use, treatment utilization and substance use, and gender and sensation-seeking differences in substance use.

When searching for a topic for my dissertation, I attempted to merge my identities as a researcher and clinician. Consequently, I have a dissertation goal of documenting the differential effects of rape among addicted women on treatment utilization, treatment motivation, perceived barriers to treatment, and problem severity. I believe that there is a lack of research and knowledge of the difference rape makes in treatment for women in the addiction field. The purpose of my dissertation is twofold. First, I intend to show that rape decreases motivation for addiction treatment, causes more perceived barriers to treatment, decreases treatment utilization, and increases different types of problem severity. Second, I intend to explore some qualitative questions regarding their motivation for treatment. The latter section intends to explore more of the interplay of their symptoms and their motivation for various types of treatment. The main motivation construct in this study is based on Prochaska and DiClemente's model. I have chosen to apply for a grant to fund my project and to utilize a publication format for my dissertation write-up, and I intend to have at least two manuscripts suitable for publication as an end result.

I have developed a strong knowledge base in statistical and research methodology as a result of my educational career. I have worked on many research projects, performing a myriad of duties ranging from working with participants, to data entry, to questionnaire development, to data analysis. Consequently, I have developed a strong research identity. Additionally, as a scientist–practitioner, I believe that research should inform clinical practice and clinical practice should inform research. Therefore, I am committed to publishing and presenting results of my psychological research at national and local conferences. I am currently working on multiple manuscripts that will be submitted for publication prior to my beginning internship. In addition, I am committed to publishing the results of my dissertation. I am dedicated to presenting and publishing my work because I believe it will provide valuable information to clinicians and other researchers.

As someone who aspires to future research in trauma, posttraumatic stress, and substance use, as related to treatment engagement, completion, and efficacy, I believe I can further develop my research skills through additional research and clinical mentorship. Therefore, I continuously seek clinical and research experiences related to these interests to help inform my research *and clinical future.*

Sample Essay 4C. My research focuses broadly on the etiologies, assessment, and treatment of impulsive, aggressive, and self-injurious behaviors in children and adolescents. These behaviors are widespread and often cause serious impairment and physical harm, yet they are not well studied or understood, particularly in children and adolescents. Given the limited research on these topics to date, much of my research has attempted to answer fundamental questions related to the development and assessment of these conditions. For instance, my master's thesis examined affective, behavioral, and cognitive aspects of child suicide. Other studies I have completed examined more extreme forms of impulsive and aggressive behavior such as parent-directed physical aggression in clinic-referred children and severe acts of violence in Vietnam veterans.

Although these and other studies of mine have explored a range of factors associated with aggressive and self-injurious behaviors, I have become particularly interested in the role of emotion dysregulation in the occurrence of these behaviors. For instance, I found that the primary reason given for self-mutilation by adolescent psychiatric inpatients is that it serves to help regulate their emotional experiences. Also, frustration intolerance, a related construct, was a significant predictor of parent-directed physical aggression in children in another study. The significant role of emotion dysregulation in the occurrence of aggressive and self-injurious behaviors has led to a secondary interest in other conditions characterized by problems with emotion regulation, such as anxiety and depressive disorders. Obviously, there is still much work to be done in addressing fundamental questions related to the assessment and prediction of impulsive, aggressive, and self-injurious behaviors, as well as on emotion dysregulation, and one arm of my research will continue to focus in these areas.

More recently, the scope of my research has expanded to focus on the treatment of impulsive and aggressive behaviors in children and adolescents. I completed a second master's thesis that included a review of recent progress in the treatment of child conduct problems and concluded that there is a significant gap in our understanding of the mechanisms through which these treatments work or what factors moderate their efficacy or effectiveness. My dissertation, for which I received an NIMH National Research Service Award, is addressing one factor that pertains to the latter issue: namely, the role of parents' participation (i.e., attendance and adherence) in their child's treatment. More specifically, I am conducting (a) a descriptive study examining several potential predictors (e.g., parent motivation and expectancies for treatment) and outcomes of parent participation, as well as (b) a randomized, controlled clinical trial testing a brief (one-session) intervention designed to increase parent participation by identifying and removing potential barriers to parent participation at the start of treatment. At a very basic level, the efficacy of our current treatments—particularly those that are skills based—may be weakened if clients do not attend or adhere to treatment. Accordingly, this line of research may produce a means of improving the therapeutic outcome of a range of clinical conditions and client populations.

Given my interest in continuing these, and related, lines of clinical research, I am extremely excited about the possibility of participating in the [Site] child and adolescent internship program. Several of the clinical rotations offered, such as those at the Institute for the Study of Psychological Service and the Anxiety and Mood Disorders Service, as well as the opportunity to work in the psychiatric inpatient unit, match closely with my goals for clinical training as well as with my current and future research interests.

COVER LETTER: "SELL" THE FIT

The cover letter is an introduction to you and your application file, so it should not be a generic form letter. This is your first chance to set a tone and reveal some of your personality and professionalism through your writing style. Your cover letter provides a quick overview of your application packet and is the perfect opportunity to share information that may not otherwise fit within the AAPI or essays. Some argue that your cover letter may be the most important part of your application because it primes the reader for everything else that follows. Therefore, your cover letter should be professional, well organized, and well written.

A cover letter often begins with a paragraph indicating the name of the site and the rotation(s) to which you are applying, a list of materials included in the application file, and a list of any additional materials that were requested. In subsequent paragraphs, you will discuss the fit between your goals and the training experiences available at the site. More on this below.

When writing the body of this letter, think of the text as an abstract of your application. In other words, make sure to highlight the main themes and points but do not provide rote information that is explicitly listed in your AAPI, on your CV. Thus, you should provide broad summary statements that give the reader a general picture of who you are and what you would like him or her to focus on when reviewing the rest of your application.

Also, some applicants appropriately have used the cover letter to make the admissions committee aware of any personal reason they may have for relocation. This is certainly not required, but, for example, if you are looking for an opportunity to tell the committee that you would really like to return to your hometown next year, then this may be the place to do it. Or, you may wish to let the committee know that you would seriously consider relocation (e.g., "I am looking forward to the possibility of moving to Honolulu") to help convey your interest in the site. This may be especially important for programs that are in less desirable locations and want to ensure that applicants would actually consider them if they are a good fit. However, if you do discuss your reasons for relocation, be sure that you do so in a way that conveys that location is only one of many reasons that you are interested in a program. Otherwise, the selection committee may be left thinking that you are applying primarily because you want to live in that geographic area and not because the program is a good fit for your training goals.

"Selling" the Fit

If the cover letter is the only place in your application materials in which you are discussing your training goals and how you perceive that these goals fit the opportunities offered at the training site, then you need to go back and revise Essays 1 through 4! The cover letter should serve as a brief statement of your training goals and a more specific articulation of the exact rotations, didactic seminars, philosophies, supervisors, and other site qualities that directly fit your interests.

Unlike the four essays, the cover letter needs to be tailored for each individual program to which you are applying.

- *Use strong language.* If you think that this site is a unique or exceptional match, then say so. Convince the reader that training at his or her site would be ideal to help you achieve your specific training goals.
- *List rotations/experiences.* Yes, this will mean that you will need to rewrite this statement, in part or whole, for each application. However, if the essays generally state your goals for training overall, then the cover letter may be the only document that you need to substantially revise for each site. It is a good idea to list the rotations and experiences that are of greatest interest. You do not have to commit to anything, but instead make clear that several exciting opportunities match your interests, and you easily could be happy with a combination of the experiences offered at the site. Don't state that "everything at your site sounds great!" because that does not suggest a specific match.
- *Be authentic.* Do not state a fit if there is not one. Remember, you are looking for not just a slot, but the best fit. If you say you are interested in something that you are not, or if you exaggerate the level of your interest, you are doing a disservice not only to the site and the other applicants but also most certainly to yourself. Interestingly, many applicants report that they write their first cover letter to the site that they are most interested in, and then in descending order of interest thereafter. By application number 10 or so, many applicants realize that they are having a hard time writing a compelling fit argument in their cover letter and decide not to apply to some of these poorer-fit sites after all. This is good. If you don't see a fit, neither will the site!
- *Be enthusiastic!* You have been in the same graduate program for at least 3 (maybe 10?) years. This is a chance to go out into the world and establish a professional identity beyond the walls of your school. This is the beginning of everything that led you to pursue graduate training so many years ago. Sure,

you may be tired now, distressed about your dissertation, and worried about obtaining an internship match. Yes, you may have questioned your career choice several times over the past 3 or more rigorous years of training. But now you are almost there, and your career is about to change forever. Remember how excited you were when you were admitted to graduate school and thought about a career as a practitioner, researcher, consultant, or teacher? Reclaim that enthusiasm, if only for a moment! And then write the letter.

SUMMARY   Many applicants view the AAPI essays and the cover letter as major roadblocks to completing applications for internship. Indeed, the task of writing five stories about your personal and professional selves can be intimidating. By clarifying your professional goals prior to starting the essays, you can connect those short stories into one longer, more powerful story, and you can increase the likelihood of communicating your fit with internship sites.

Once you have written a stellar and compelling set of essays and your cover letter, it is time to think about your supplementary materials and your approach to the interview process; these are discussed in the next two chapters.

Sample Cover Letter

Dear Dr. X:

Thank you for reviewing my application to the predoctoral internship training program at the Lady Training Clinic (LTC). I am a clinical psychology doctoral candidate in my fifth year at the University of MTV. I believe my interests and graduate training experiences make me an excellent candidate for your internship program. Included with this letter, please find the AAPI Online Application, graduate transcript, CV, and four letters of recommendation.

Consistent with the ideals of the scientist–practitioner model, I am committed to a career that combines and, thus, mutually enriches clinical practice, teaching, and clinically relevant research. Overall, I am extremely interested in the program at LTC because it would allow me to further develop as a versatile and competent clinician, as well as a productive researcher. Moreover, I am drawn to your program's dual emphasis on evidence-based practice and applied research to inform the development and implementation of future treatments. Based on your program materials, reputation, and the report of a current trainee, I believe that your program is ideally suited to my accomplishing my primary training goals. Each of these is outlined below.

First, I wish to continue to develop broad-based competencies in conducting assessment and therapy with populations that are diverse in terms of developmental stages, clinical presentations, and multicultural backgrounds and identities. As such, I am thrilled by the unparalleled opportunity afforded to each intern at LTC to collaboratively develop an individual training program. My intention would be to take full advantage of this flexibility, first by advancing my emerging specialization in working with children, adolescents, and families across a variety of inpatient and outpatient rotations. Additionally, my clinical and research endeavors to date have taught me to appreciate the compelling utility of a developmental, life-span psychopathology perspective. Accordingly, I am equally committed to further developing my intervention and assessment skills with adult populations. I am excited by your program's opportunities to gain general clinical training through a wide variety of Adult Rotations.

Second, I am excited by the unique opportunity LTC would offer for me to balance a breadth of clinical experiences with more focused training in areas of emerging specialization. My clinical and research interests concentrate on adolescent anxiety and shared mechanisms of emotion dysregulation. For example, I am currently performing crisis evaluations with adolescents and parents participating in an NIMH-funded study of adolescent OCD. I wish to continue to deepen and expand my assessment and intervention skills with high-risk populations. I would be thrilled by the opportunity to gain advanced training in the Assessment and Treatment of Adolescent Anxiety Disorders program, as well as in the psychiatric emergency room of the Diagnostic Evaluation Center.

Third, and relatedly, given my deep commitment to the integration of science and practice in my career, I wish to gain additional research training and experiences on internship and beyond. I will have defended my dissertation project in advance of my internship year and, as such, I would be interested in pursuing additional, independent research opportunities with several of your research preceptors. In particular, I would be excited to continue my research in the area of adolescent anxiety under the mentorship of Dr. Beyonce. I believe that the experience of conducting clinical research at LTC would be integral in preparing me for a practice and research-oriented career within an urban, academic medical center.

Fourth, to more effectively address a full spectrum of clinical presentations, I wish to enhance my solid grounding in CBT case formulation and intervention with continued exposure to empirically supported treatments. Accordingly, the LTC program's explicit commitment to the application of evidence-based practice is an obvious draw. As well, I seek continued supervision in the application of integrated theoretical models of psychotherapy to meet the unique needs and preferences of each individual client. I am excited by your program's opportunities to receive supervision in several therapeutic modalities and theoretical orientations, including CBT, DBT, and IPT approaches.

Finally, and on a more personal level, my partner and I are hoping to return to Honolulu for internship. I am from Hawaii and several of my immediate family members and friends still reside there. Training at LTC would allow me to benefit from the phenomenal training opportunities at your site while enabling me to return to the region of the country where I hope to establish myself professionally.

Thank you again for considering my application. Should you have any questions, please do not hesitate to contact me by phone. I look forward to hearing from you.

Best regards,

Your Name

4 CURRICULUM VITAE AND LETTERS OF RECOMMENDATION

You have calculated your hours, entered information into your APPIC Application for Psychology Internships (AAPI), and written thoughtful essays and a cover letter that truly reflect your training and career goals. The next steps in the application process are to put together your curriculum vitae (CV) and to request letters of recommendation.

Ultimately, the manner in which you prepare these materials will be based on your own professional style and personal preferences. To help you prepare these documents, this chapter offers some guidelines regarding their purpose and most effective uses. Remember that your application folder usually will be reviewed in its entirety; thus, you will want all of your materials to fit together as a package that compellingly sells you as an internship applicant.

YOUR CURRICULUM VITAE

Internship sites expect that you will submit a CV with your application and not a résumé. A résumé is a concise (usually one or two pages) snapshot of you and your qualifications for a particular job, whereas a CV is more comprehensive (for most applicants, between five and 10 pages) and can be thought of as an evolving document. Keep in mind that your CV is a tool to inform and persuade; thus, it should be written in a compelling, accurate manner. The CV is also a reflection of who you are. Hence, you want to be sure that it is error free and easy to read and understand.

You should write your CV with your particular professional audience in mind. In this case, your audience includes internship training directors and faculty. Therefore, you should try to emphasize your clinical experiences and competencies but also be economical with your use of words; be consistent with your style, grammar, and tense; and use the active voice. A sloppy CV may be interpreted as indicative of a sloppy clinician.

DOI: 10.1037/13946-004
Internships in Psychology: The APAGS Workbook for Writing Successful Applications and Finding the Right Fit, Third Edition, by C. Williams-Nickelson, M. J. Prinstein, and W. G. Keilin

A CV with excessive use of fonts, underscoring, and graphics may be more helpful when applying for a job in computer science than one in psychology.

Years ago, people tended to include a lot of personal information on their CVs, including photographs. However, this is rarely done anymore, and we strongly recommend that you not include a picture, your date of birth, the number of children you have, your height and weight, your hobbies, your astrological sign, or similar items. These inclusions are likely to be interpreted as offering too much information or as "padding" your CV with unnecessary material. Other common but questionable text includes information about where you attended high school, that you were the captain of your college football team, or that you won a beauty contest. Although some training directors may be interested in hearing about these things, we think that it is better to save this personal information for a conversation rather than to categorize these as academic achievements on your CV.

Other examples of unnecessary or redundant material that people commonly include on their CVs are class presentations, the names of conferences attended, published abstracts, and so forth. Most sites will ask for a transcript that already documents your coursework, so, unless you have a specific purpose for including class presentations or naming the conferences you attended, it is usually best to leave them out of your CV. It is expected that as a graduate student you will have given many class presentations and should be fairly competent in this area. On the other hand, if you attended special seminars or workshops, or became certified in a particular area or technique that is relevant to the sites to which you are applying, it would be perfectly appropriate to include that information on your CV. Finally, as with everything else, give your CV to others to review.

Usually, a desire to create a lengthy CV originates from a concern that one has too few accomplishments or may be evaluated as underqualified. Remember that you are applying for a training position; thus, you need to demonstrate that you are "trainable," which means that you are not expected to have a lengthy list of accomplishments. If the director of clinical training in your graduate program says that you are ready to apply for internship, then you probably are!

Constructing Your CV

The following list of dos and don'ts offers overarching strategies that will help you develop a CV that is effective in presenting your experiences and skills in a professional manner.

- *Do* know the difference between a résumé and a CV. You should submit a CV with your internship application. A *résumé* is a concise, business-style report that displays your job qualifications to a prospective employer. It is usually one to two pages long; reflects basic information about education, work experience, volunteerism, awards, and publications; includes a statement of goals, purpose, or objectives; and lists specific skills, achievements, and education and training accomplishments that make you a likely candidate for a specific job. It is a snapshot of your employment experience. On the other hand, a CV is unlimited in length and is an evolving document that includes information covered on a résumé, without the statement of goals, purpose, or objectives. A CV records more descriptive information about education, training, work experience, volunteerism, awards, publications, presentations, demonstration of leadership or professional service, research, and the like. It is a comprehensive picture of you. *Curriculum vitae* is, after all, Latin for the "course of (one's) life."

- *Do* understand that you will probably have to edit several drafts of your CV to make it clearer, more concise, and increasingly polished. Even though your CV is endlessly perfectible, *don't* require yourself to create a perfect document.
- *Do* ask trusted faculty members to review your CV and provide you with feedback about its content and organization.
- *Do* avoid jargon and slang, but *don't* confuse discipline-specific language (i.e., the specialized language psychologists use) with jargon. Discipline-specific language is the shortest, clearest, and most appropriate way to communicate within psychology, and it is fine to use psychology terminology in your CV.
- *Do* remember that the purpose of your CV is to inform and persuade.
- *Do* tell your CV readers what they need to know, and place information in an order that is most useful to them.
- *Do* think about the audience for which you are preparing your CV. For example, consider the type of site to which you are applying (e.g., counseling center, Veterans Affairs, medical center). How much does your audience know about your experiences (i.e., your program, your practica, your work experience, your professional involvement)? What questions can you anticipate from your audience (and address in your CV)? Have you omitted any significant information that the audience needs?
- *Do* remember that, depending on experience, education, mind-sets, and conceptual frameworks, every CV reader will react differently to the same words on a page, and you will not have complete control over audience responses.
- *Do* present the facts without distortion.
- *Do* remember that an economy of words is desirable; complete sentences are not necessary.
- *Do* use lists whenever appropriate.
- *Do* use topic headings to increase organization and ease of readability.
- *Do* keep lists consistent in grammatical form (all verbs or all nouns or noun forms or all complete sentences). Use the active voice as much as possible. Use present and past tenses appropriately. Vary word choice (find synonyms for overused words like *provide*) and keep it simple (e.g., *use* is better than *utilize*).
- *Don't* include your date or place of birth, height and weight, health condition, relationship status, hobbies or interests, religion, type of automobile you drive, favorite color, astrological sign, or similar information. Remember, this is a document to help you gain a professional position, not to help you find a date.
- *Don't* offer information just because you have it—it may be unnecessary and even unhelpful (e.g., name of high school, elementary school penmanship awards, cheerleading experience). Inclusion of this information is certainly your choice, but think about the possible interpretations and implications.
- *Don't* include a picture.
- *Do* tactfully acknowledge your skills by describing what you have done and what you do rather than using broad and vague adjectives or pretentious, obscure, and esoteric language. For example, the words *responsible, intelligent,*

and *committed* are too vague. Describe how you have been responsible. Offer information that will help the reader see that you are intelligent. Discuss projects or activities you have been involved with and seen through to the end to demonstrate commitment. As another example, referring to the act of smelling something as "olfactory analysis" is unnecessarily obscure. Be vivid and precise.

- *Do* use active versus passive voice.
- *Do* remember that your CV is your written portrait. Like your personal appearance in a face-to-face interview, the physical appearance, or format, of your CV is important, testifying to your initiative, ability to communicate, and overall professionalism. It helps people know what you have to offer; it is an extension of you. Your personality and work style will be judged by the presentation of your CV.
- *Do* make yourself memorable by the overall quality, organization, and content of your CV.

Organizing Your CV

The information on your CV should be organized into logical groupings. Following is an outline and discussion of the major areas of the CV in a natural progressive order of information.

1. Name, Address, Telephone and Fax Number(s) With Area Code, and E-Mail Address
   - Position this information at the top of the first page.
   - Place last name and page number at the top or bottom of every additional page.
   - Use a permanent address and telephone number; you may list both a home and a work number.
2. Education
   - List the entries in chronological order.
   - List the name, location (city, state), degree earned, graduation date, major(s), cumulative GPAs (optional), and GPAs in major (optional) for each university and degree.
   - List honors, scholarships, and awards either with each institution or under a separate category.
   - Do not include high school, as it is generally not necessary.
   - Include information about all undergraduate and graduate programs that you attended, even if some are in fields that are unrelated to psychology and even if your attendance did not result in your obtaining a degree.
3. Employment (if applicable)
   - List entries in chronological order, starting with the most recent job.
   - Include the agency's name, department (if appropriate), and the city and state. You may also choose to list your immediate supervisor's name, if desired.
   - Do not report salary information.
   - List the last position or job title you held.
   - List your dates of employment from month/year to month/year.
   - Include a narrative or bulleted points that describe your specific duties, including workload, type of work, level of responsibility, supervision provided to

others, programs developed or administered, special projects, achievements, promotions, positions held that led to current position, and any budgetary responsibilities (use active voice and avoid vague adjectives).
- Include work awards and commendations.
- Do not include your reason for leaving the position.

Example:
PacifiCare, Inc.   Oct. 1997–Present
Somewhere North, CA   *Supervisor:* Martin Evil, MBA

Position: Claims Reviewer and Authorizer

Responsibilities: Provide consultation to physicians in developing insurance-approved treatment plans; authorize laboratory work and medical testing based on insurer's benefit plan and medical need; complete quarterly cost-benefit analyses; and specialize in behavioral health services.

4. Volunteer or Service Work
   - Format this section similar to the employment section with name, mailing address, area code and telephone number, supervisor or volunteer coordinator, and dates of service.
   - Include an official title, if applicable.
   - Report responsibilities.
5. Practica or Psychotherapy Experience
   - Format this section similar to the employment and volunteer sections.
   - Include the names of all supervisors.
   - Specify type of services, population served, special treatment protocol and interventions used, amount of testing, consultation, multidisciplinary team work, average time spent weekly or monthly at the site, range of presenting problems, psychotropic medication management, and other services provided.

Example:
Friendly Medical Center   Sept. 1996–Present
Department of Behavioral Medicine   *Supervisor:* Sandy Stressfree, PhD
Somewhere North, CA

Responsibilities: Provide health psychology services to a range of patients with cognitive impairment, high blood pressure, chronic pain, and depression; complete neuropsychological assessments; provide individual and group therapy to patients and their family members; work as part of an interdisciplinary team with psychiatrists, physicians, nurses, social workers, and rehabilitation therapists in the urology, cardiac, surgical recovery, and orthopedic departments; use hypnotherapy and cognitive behavior therapy interventions; conduct standardized smoking cessation programs; and participate in grand rounds.

Hours: Approximately 20 hours per week.

6. Provision of Supervision (if applicable)
   - Describe your supervisory experience and style.
   - Describe the type of supervision offered (e.g., live, group, individual, videotaped, audiotaped).
   - List supervisee characteristics (e.g., provided supervision to social workers, master's counseling students; primarily supervised couples therapy cases).
7. Professional Affiliations and Leadership Roles
   - List all memberships in professional associations.
   - List level of membership (e.g., affiliate, student, associate, full), and make sure you are documenting this correctly.
   - Indicate membership duration.
   - Describe the professional organization if it is not commonly known.
   - List any offices, roles, or projects associated with professional organization membership or involvement.
   - List special committee memberships (e.g., advisory board, steering committee, school senate).
8. Awards and Scholarships
   - List the name of the award or scholarship, who nominated, who bestowed, type of award or scholarship, and date conferred. (There are very few universally recognized and understood awards and scholarships, so you need to describe what you won and why you won it.)
   - Indicate dollar amounts for awards or scholarships if they are substantial or provide important information.
   - Do not include awards that are not meaningful (e.g., "Listed in the Who's Who Among Psychology Graduate Students").
9. Licensure
   - Include any licenses you hold, the name of the licensing board, the date the license was obtained, and your license number.
10. Teaching Experience
    - List the name of university, department, mailing address, dates of teaching, and supervisor(s) names in a format similar to the employment listings.
    - Indicate the name and level of the course(s) you taught and the number of times each course was taught at each institution.
11. Research
    - List your research projects as well as your dissertation research.
    - Include details about the nature of your research involvement. (Do you work with participants, analyze data, train research assistants to administer particular assessments?)
    - Include the names of your research supervisor(s), dissertation chair, and purpose of the research (i.e., research assistant, significant class project).
12. Grants
    - List the title of the project, name of the funding agency, and dates of the funding.
    - List your role on the grant (PI, Co-Pi; Co-I, Consultant).
    - Include the dollar amount of the grant (optional).
13. Professional Presentations
    - List presentations at professional conferences and workshops.
    - Use the most recent American Psychological Association (APA) Style.

14. Publications
    - List any publications and manuscripts in print, in press, under review, and (perhaps) in preparation.
    - Use the most recent APA Style.
    - List only articles in professional publications (i.e., not in the school newspaper or supermarket circular unless you have a deliberate reason for doing so).
15. Other Sections (if applicable)
    - Do not list continuing education workshops that you have attended or special presentations that you have attended at national, state, or local conferences, as most CV reviewers do not find this information useful or enhancing. In fact, it could be interpreted as padding your CV and thus could detract from your substantive work.
    - List conferences attended only if you have a specific reason (e.g., to document specialty training) for including this information (and make that reason clear to the reviewer).
    - List special courses only if you have a specific reason (e.g., to document unique certification of skills) for including this information (and make that reason clear to the reviewer). Your internship site will usually have your transcripts, and if they do not ask for your transcripts to be included with your application materials, they generally are not interested in reviewing a list of your classes. Thus, you should not include such a list on your CV.
16. References
    - Be sure to check with references before providing their names and contact information to others, and try to alert them of any potential calls ahead of time.
    - Give your references your CV and other information to make it easy for them to highlight your outstanding accomplishments.

LETTERS OF RECOMMENDATION

Most applicants can secure positive letters of recommendation that attest to clinical competence and internship readiness. This is expected. However, what sets your recommendation letters apart from other letters is evidence of the following:

1. You are genuinely liked and respected by your peers, faculty, and supervisors.
2. You consistently demonstrate professionalism.
3. You can work well with others—your peers, your supervisors, and your subordinates. You are collegial and respectful.
4. You are committed to learning; even though you may enter the internship with impressive skills, you are interested in expanding those skills.
5. You are responsible, responsive, and hardworking, and you complete high-quality work.
6. You are a leader.
7. You are invested in the profession.
8. You are *normal*.

Your goal is to obtain recommendation letters that offer the most accurate and positive description of your skills, accomplishments, and personal demeanor. When you ask someone for a letter, specifically ask, "Can you write a *strong* letter of support?" If that individual answers yes without hesitation, then you can assume that his or her letter will be helpful. If that person expresses any reservations, you should ask someone else.

Applicants often wonder about strategies for gathering recommendation letters from particular psychologists. They ask, "What if two of my supervisors from the same practicum site write me letters? Does this make it seem like my other practicum supervisors cannot write strong letters?" "What if all of my letters are from junior faculty?" "Will it increase my chances of being ranked high if I have 'high-profile' psychologists write my letters?"

Our advice is that you try not to worry about any other strategy except getting strong letters from people who know you and your work very well. Oftentimes, the "high-profile psychologist" letters do not impress internship sites, unless these psychologists can speak in-depth about your clinical and personal skills. If you have the choice between sending a weak letter from a "big-name" psychologist versus a very strong letter from a junior faculty member, we recommend that you ask the junior faculty member to write the letter.

Some people also wonder whether it is advisable to solicit a letter of recommendation from a nonpsychologist (e.g., a physician, psychiatrist, social worker). Although such professionals may be able to comment on your ability to work in a multidisciplinary setting, it is less likely that they will be able to comment on the types of skills and competencies that are expected of doctoral-level psychologists; therefore, it may be better to obtain letters exclusively from psychologists. On the other hand, if a nonpsychologist knows you well and fully understands the range of professional capabilities that should be addressed in a letter of recommendation for psychology internships, this person may be in an excellent position to be one of your recommenders.

And under no circumstances should you ever ask for a letter from your therapist! Your therapist cannot speak to your clinical skills, although he or she can talk about you in clinical terms. Similarly, letters from individuals with whom your relationship is primarily personal rather than professional, or from individuals who cannot speak directly to your skills as a psychologist-in-training, should be avoided.

You should begin cultivating relationships with potential letter writers now. Make appointments to talk with your advisor, supervisors, and other faculty members whom you might ask to write letters. Provide the psychologist with a copy of your CV. Discuss your research ideas. Discuss your practica experiences. Tell him or her about your previous jobs, volunteer work, and leadership activities. Most important, tell him or her about your goals for training on internship. In short, give these psychologists information about yourself that will help them form an accurate and comprehensive professional and personal opinion of you so that they will have the necessary information to write a strong recommendation letter when the time comes.

Discuss your growth areas with your letter writers so that they can integrate these into your recommendation letters. We all have growth areas. If your letter writers can talk about your ability to think introspectively about your areas for growth and the steps you have already taken to address them, it speaks volumes to your ability to receive and incorporate feedback, as well as your interest in developing your skills.

The ability to speak to the strength of your character is also important in recommendation letters. Sites want to know what type of a person you are, because they will have to work with you for at least a year.

Exhibit 4.1.   *Sample Request for Recommendation Letter*

LETTER WRITER:	Brooke Shields, PhD
APPLICANT NAME:	Tom Cruise, MA
PERSONAL CONTACTS:	9/2005–8/2006: Postpartum Depression Practicum 6/2007–present: Advanced Practicum
APPLYING TO INTERNSHIP SITES:	1. Veterans Affairs Medical Center 2. Hollywood Medical Center, Psychiatry Dept. 3. Mission Impossible Hospital, Dept. of Psychology 4. Cocktail Consortium 5. Far Away School of Medicine/Psychiatry 6. Magnolia Consortium 7. The Firm Health Sciences Center, Charleston, WV
PLEASE HIGHLIGHT AS YOU DEEM APPROPRIATE:	1. My level of enthusiasm and motivation. 2. Ability to connect with clients and create a therapeutic alliance. 3. My clinical skills, including case conceptualization, treatment planning, and treatment implementation. 4. Interest in learning a treatment modality that incorporates my research interests. 5. My ability to work with a patient with a trauma history. (Brooke—I'm really interested in continuing to work with trauma on internship. All of the places I'm applying to have major rotations that involve PTSD treatment, and you are the only supervisor who is in a position to comment on my ability to work with clients who have a history of trauma.) 6. My ability to balance acceptance and change strategies with my clients (I am thinking about the comorbid client we worked on together as a good example of this).
PLEASE SEND LETTER TO ME BY:	October 15, 2007
SEE ATTACHED FOR COPIES OF:	Curriculum vitae and past practicum evaluation

Applicants may give letter writers a Request for Recommendation Letter sheet (see sample form, Exhibit 4.1) that indicates the kind of information the letter should contain. Some letter writers may find it helpful, but be aware that others may interpret this gesture as you telling them what to say. You will know your letter writers and their preferences best. Ask them how you can be most helpful to them in providing any information in any format that will make their letter writing as easy as possible. Remember, too, that in most cases it is understood to be the job of your clinical supervisors to write internship recommendation letters, so this should not be a surprise to them. However, also remember that they are likely to have many letters to write, so be respectful of their time by providing them with plenty of time to compose your letter. Do not underestimate the time it takes to write a thoughtful and helpful recommendation letter.

Finally, do not send more letters than a site requests. Additional letters are not going to convey anything the first three to four strong letters have not already conveyed.

If you send extra letters, at best, they will be ignored. At worst, it will demonstrate that you do not know how to follow directions.

ADDITIONAL SITE-SPECIFIC MATERIALS

In about one in 10 cases, sites may ask you to include a work sample, an additional essay question, or some other type of additional information to help them in their selection process. If this is the case, work with your director of clinical training to determine which work sample should be included and how it should be presented to conceal the identity of the client, if relevant. Your director of clinical training can also provide you with tips about how to answer additional essay questions.

SUMMARY

The materials discussed in this chapter include a CV, recommendation letters, and any unique materials that are site specific. Together, these materials will convey your experience, interests, and professionalism, and perhaps also some of your personal characteristics. Now that you have prepared and submitted your applications, it is time to rest. In only a few weeks, you should start hearing from sites about interviews—the subject of the next chapter.

5 THE INTERVIEW

Submitting your application materials is an accomplishment worthy of celebration and much relief. This milestone also begins a sometimes agonizing waiting period that ends once you receive your first decision notification regarding interviews. Sites vary considerably in the proportion of applicants they invite for an interview. Although some sites invite all applicants for a visit, you can expect that most sites will extend invitations to five to 10 applicants for every available internship slot. This chapter covers the basic information needed to successfully manage the interview process.

SCHEDULING INTERVIEWS

You can expect to hear from internship sites about interview decisions in late November through early January. Most interviews occur in December and January. Some sites allow you to select the date of your visit from many choices, whereas others may have only one or two dates to interview all invited applicants. Scheduling interviews can be a logistical challenge, and it is sometimes necessary and permissible to call an internship site to ask whether you have been invited for an interview there so that you can coordinate travel plans. (*Note:* Be nice to administrative assistants! They're trying as hard as they can, and they tell the faculty *everything!*) Remember that Association of Psychology Postdoctoral and Internship Centers (APPIC)–member sites must list in the *APPIC Directory* the date by which they will notify all applicants as to whether or not they are still being considered and will be invited for an interview. APPIC also has suggested that all sites notify applicants of their interview decisions by December 15. Having this information allows you to make travel plans and other decisions about interviews. Be sure to allow for at least one day to regroup between each interview; the itineraries can be quite exhausting.

DOI: 10.1037/13946-005
Internships in Psychology: The APAGS Workbook for Writing Successful Applications and Finding the Right Fit, Third Edition, by C. Williams-Nickelson, M. J. Prinstein, and W. G. Keilin

Interview Formats

Expect a range of interview formats, which are usually influenced by how a site defines and prefers to assess the fit between candidates and the site.

Open house "interviews." Some sites welcome all applicants to visit the internship site as part of an open house. These open houses generally are optional and informal. For many sites, attendance at the open house is not mandatory and may not increase your chances of being selected. Often the open house is not a true interview; it is simply an opportunity for you to visit the site to obtain information about a program that could not be conveyed in a brochure or by telephone. Some may not even ask you to wear name tags, to emphasize that they are not evaluating you during the open house at all. You may find it difficult to schedule one-on-one interviews with potential supervisors during the open house meeting. Sites that offer open houses will typically follow up with formal in-person or telephone interviews.

Telephone interviews. Some sites conduct telephone interviews exclusively, whereas others may offer a telephone interview to applicants who are unable to schedule an in-person interview for whatever reason. Many applicants have successfully matched at sites at which they have been able to participate in only a telephone rather than an in-person interview. This is a reasonable option for those applicants unable to travel to a site, although obviously it is not possible to view the facility without the in-person visit.

Telephone interviews usually last from 30 minutes to 1 hour. They are usually conducted by the training director and one or more staff psychologists involved in training. The current interns tend not to be involved in telephone interviews, although they may be, depending on the site. Many telephone interviews are structured. That is, all candidates are asked the same questions in the same order and manner. You will not have the opportunity to gauge your responses on the basis of interviewer nonverbal feedback, but there are many advantages to telephone interviews. You can wear whatever you want. You can take copious notes and use the program brochure or website without worrying about making sufficient eye contact and remaining visibly engaged. There is quite a bit of scheduling flexibility, and there are no travel costs.

Site visits/in-person interviews. A large majority of interviews occur in person at the internship site. The structure of the interviews can vary considerably and will range from standardized to free-flowing conversation. Group interviews, including multiple applicants and faculty members, are possible, as are one-on-one interviews that last 30 to 60 minutes, or some combination of the two. Some of your interviews will be very structured; you may be asked a series of standardized questions to assess the breadth and depth of your clinical experience. Other interviews may be extremely informal; in fact, interviews may consist of friendly conversation with a supervisor about topics unrelated to psychology. Still other interviews may focus entirely on questions that you have about the site, requiring you to maintain the conversation and fill the interview time with many good questions. Over the years, the most common piece of feedback we have heard from applicants is that they were surprised at how much they were expected to ask the questions on interviews, rather than be asked. Your meetings may take place in a faculty member's office, while you are touring the facility, or during a lunch. You may even have the chance to explore the facility on your own. Some sites will have a full day of interviews scheduled for you, with meetings from breakfast through the end of the day. Other sites may schedule only two or three appointments with faculty or interns. Whatever the format, remember that you are being evaluated every moment you are at the site. Therefore, pay attention to how you treat support staff and your colleagues who are also interviewing. Many sites provide information about how they interview in their listing within the *APPIC Directory*.

Interview Checklist: Before You Go

- It is a good idea to bring along a copy of the site materials on your interview so that you may review them before beginning the interview day. Interviewers usually prefer to spend the meeting time discussing information that you could not have obtained from their site brochure. A quick review of the site materials will also help remind you of the experiences that made you most interested in the site when you applied.
- A review of your application also is helpful before beginning the interview day. You will undoubtedly be asked to discuss your perceptions regarding the fit between your interests and the training opportunities at the site. It is best to review the points you stated in your cover letter to prepare for this question.
- In many cases, you will know more about the training site than each interviewer knows about you. Bring along a few copies of your curriculum vitae (CV)—you may be asked for them. Do not assume that those interviewing you will remember your application materials well, will have read them recently, or even at all! Do not be offended by this. Simply introduce yourself anew and with the same enthusiasm you had when you submitted your application materials.
- Sites that emphasize research as well as clinical training might offer an opportunity to meet with a potential research supervisor. Much as you did when applying for graduate programs, you may want to review potential supervisors' research abstracts to help you develop informed questions regarding their work. Keep in mind that for most clinical internships, including many research-oriented internship sites, a thorough review of supervisors' research is not necessary.
- Many applicants have questions regarding appropriate attire for the internship interview. The answer is simple: Dress professionally—whatever that means for you. As a benchmark, it may be helpful to know that most male applicants wear a jacket and tie on the interview day; many wear a suit. Female applicants should consider wearing a dress or suit, dress shoes (with hosiery), and small jewelry. Dress as you would if you were on a job interview (you are!). However, it is important that you be comfortable and genuine. Resist the urge to wear an item of clothing or jewelry that will help you to "stand out" from among the other applicants; instead, attempt to differentiate yourself on the basis of your qualifications, social skills, enthusiasm, and unique fit with the site.
- Perhaps most important, review the site materials (or website) thoroughly before you attend the interview. Asking questions regarding issues that are thoroughly described on the site website sends a clear message that you are unprepared for the interview or that you are not very interested in the site. Do your homework!

Worries about internship interview etiquette often are unnecessary. Should you accept a cup of coffee if it is offered? Should your CV be printed on white or ivory paper? What's most important is thorough preparation and impressive delivery, and the ability to demonstrate good interpersonal skills. If you have been selected for an interview, you already likely possess the minimal qualifications needed to gain admission to the internship site. The interview process is a sorting process to help sites and applicants determine the extent to which there is a fit. You may often find that there is less focus on your credentials and more on your general demeanor and interests. If you effectively communicate that you are high in social skills, enthusiasm, and fit (i.e., the "Big 3"), then you have succeeded on the interview.

Social Skills

This seems obvious, and it is. Simply be appropriate, professional, and considerate. Use your clinical skills. Some interviews will be conversations about the location of the internship, about your experiences as a graduate student or about people you both know professionally. Have fun and use genuine humor! And if you get tired, remember, just be a LOSER:

> **L** – Lean forward
> **O** – Open posture—do not cross your arms over yourself
> **S** – Sit straight and squarely
> **E** – Maintain eye contact
> **R** – Relax

You may be someone with fantastic social skills in everyday life who occasionally misplaces those skills when feeling anxious. This is quite common, and otherwise congenial people become overly distracted by self-monitoring ("Did my last response sound stupid?"), intrusive thoughts ("Did I print out my boarding pass for tonight's flight?"), and simple exhaustion ("If I have to talk about my dissertation to one more person, I will have to check into this site as a patient!"). For these reasons, it is absolutely, definitely, extremely super-important that you role play, role play, role play before you begin the interview circuit.

Enthusiasm

You will likely be tired—OK, exhausted—from travel or travel delays. You may have several interviews in just a week and may find it difficult to remember the most pertinent facts about each site. You may have decided that a different site is your first choice and find it hard to appear interested in anyplace else. This is when it is most important to remember to convey enthusiasm to your hosts.

Internship sites would like to select someone who will be happy to be at their site, who will smile and have a positive attitude every day at work, and who seems energetic about the rotations and other opportunities. During the interview, let them know that you are the exact type of person they are seeking.

Following are some examples to help you convey enthusiasm.

Bad No. 1

Interviewer: Welcome to Internship X. Did you have any trouble getting here?

You: Well, my plane was canceled last night because of the storm, and I actually just flew out here at 6:00 this morning. I'm tired and angry at the airline. I always have problems with X airline. What about you? Do you hate X airline? At any rate, I hope this interview is worth it.

Better No. 1

Interviewer: Welcome to Internship X. Did you have any trouble getting here?

You: I was a little concerned with that storm yesterday, but I am excited to be here on time.

Bad No. 2

Interviewer: We do a lot of work with adults who have chronic schizophrenia. Do you have any experience with this population?

You: Actually, I don't. Will that be negotiable?

Better No. 2

Interviewer: We do a lot of work with adults who have chronic schizophrenia. Do you have any experience with this population?

You: No, I haven't had a chance to do that yet, but I think that would be a great experience for me because I realize it is important to have exposure to various treatment methodologies for severely mentally ill patients.

Bad No. 3

Interviewer: This rotation will involve a lot of assessment with children, and I see that you already have a lot of that experience. Is that something you are OK with?

You: Yeah, I guess. I figured I'd have to do more of that on internship, and that's fine if I have to do it.

Better No. 3

Interviewer: This rotation will involve a lot of assessment with children, and I see that you already have a lot of that experience. Is that something you are OK with?

You: I enjoy assessment, and I think that it would be good for me to develop that as a specialty. That sounds like it would be a great opportunity for me at this point in my training.

Fit

You must emphasize that you are a unique fit to the internship site. It is a big mistake to believe that the fit is clear or obvious simply because you have similar training experiences or because others in your graduate program previously were placed at that site. Remember that the faculty members may interview five or 10 times as many applicants as they have slots, and it is likely that they may have spent less time with your application than you have spent looking over their site materials. You need to show them the fit—explicitly. Some examples include the following:

Bad No. 1

Interviewer: What can I tell you about the rotation I supervise here at the VA?

You: Well, you tell me. What would an intern's experiences be on your rotation?

Better No. 1

Interviewer: What can I tell you about the rotation I supervise here at the VA?

You: Actually, a primary goal for me is to get experience working in a VA. I think I may want to work in this kind of position one day. So, I am particularly interested in this rotation. What would a typical intern's experience be like here?

Bad No. 2

Interviewer: Hi. You must have been asked a lot of questions already, so why don't I let you ask me something? What do you want to know?

You: OK, um, I dunno, um, do you like being here in Montana?

Better No. 2

Interviewer: Hi. You must have been asked a lot of questions already, so why don't I let you ask me something? What do you want to know?

You: OK. Well, because I am really interested in getting experience with A, B, and C on internship, I was especially excited to hear about Rotations A, B, and C. They seem to be a perfect fit with my interests and skills. I have never lived in Montana, however. What is that like?

Bad No. 3

Interviewer: You come from a behavioral program, but this rotation involves a lot of experience with the Rorschach. Do you think you will fit here?

You: I am a quick learner. I've heard the Rorschach is fairly easy, and I think I will fit just fine here.

Better No. 3

Interviewer: You come from a behavioral program, but this rotation involves a lot of experience with the Rorschach. Do you think you will fit here?

You: Interesting you should mention that. One of my goals for internship was to approach assessment from a broader perspective, so the opportunity to get Rorschach experience would be a great fit for me.

A list of sample questions that you may be asked during interviews is included in Exhibit 5.1. It may be helpful for you to construct written "talking points" to

Exhibit 5.1   *Questions You May Be Asked*

1. Tell me about yourself.
   - Break the statement down.
   - Start with professional interests and goals, but consider saying, "I'd also be happy to talk about some of my personal interests." (This shows that you are multidimensional, that is, you do have a life outside of psychology.)
2. Why did you apply to our program?
   - Outline goals and training match
   - Rotations
   - Your training experiences
   - Their setting
   - Research, if applicable
   - Any extras or unique opportunities
3. What do you want to get out of our internship (training goals)?
   - Investment in training (e.g., it fits well; you have studied their brochure, and it feels right)
   - Multidisciplinary setting—excellent training ground
   - You can make contributions (describe), plus learn, gain more experience, obtain guidance, and develop expertise.
   - Mentorship and good professional relationships with faculty
4. What things do you want to work on during internship?
5. What research would you want to pursue here?
6. What is the status of your dissertation?
7. Why did you choose clinical/counseling psychology?
8. What are the strengths of your graduate program?
9. What are the limitations of your graduate program?
10. Why should we select you as an intern? Match with program?
11. Tell me about your
    - Clinical experience
    - Assessment experience
    - Research experience
    - Most difficult client situation and how you handled it
12. What is your primary theoretical orientation? Why?
13. What would you be doing if you were not in psychology?
14. What are your personal strengths and weaknesses?
15. What are your clinical strengths and weaknesses?
16. What are your professional (collegial) strengths and weaknesses?
17. What population have you found it most difficult to work with?
18. Has any client or patient ever challenged your fundamental beliefs about life? What was that experience like? How did you manage it?
19. What are you looking for in supervision?
20. Who was your favorite supervisor? Why?
21. Who was your least favorite supervisor? Why?
22. Tell me about a negative supervisory experience.
23. Tell me about a rewarding supervisory experience.
24. How do you work with and understand people with different ethnic or cultural backgrounds?
25. Do you have a master's degree? In what?
26. What nonpsychology work experience has helped to shape your professional identity?
27. Why did you select the dissertation topic that you did?
28. Tell me about an ethical problem that you faced and how you handled it.
29. What are your future goals in psychology?
30. Where do you think the profession is heading?
31. What do you think about prescription privileges (or any other hot national psychology topic)?
32. What is your favorite or most influential psychology book?
33. What is your favorite nonpsychology book?
34. What else would you like me to know about you that is not on your CV?
35. What do you do in your spare time?
36. Tell me about your most rewarding case.
37. Tell me about your toughest case.

these questions to help crystallize your thoughts. Revisit your answers after a week or two, and determine whether they are an accurate and good reflection of you, your experiences, and your interests. Practice these responses aloud; you will be surprised to find that it is initially difficult to articulate your responses smoothly and confidently.

ASK, ASK, AND ASK AGAIN — You will be asked many questions on the interview day, and your responses will help the site get to know you better and assess their ability to provide you with meaningful and helpful training. You will also have a chance to ask questions. In fact, you will likely have more interviews during which you are the inquisitor rather than the respondent, so it is essential that you be prepared with many questions about the site. Lists of sample questions for faculty and interns are included here (see Exhibits 5.2 and 5.3, respectively), but remember that these lists may be used by many applicants—so do not ask these questions verbatim. Use this list to help generate some unique questions of your own.

The manner in which you ask these questions should capture the same themes as noted earlier and help continue to communicate that you are socially skilled, enthusiastic, and a good fit.

Examples include the following.

Bad No. 1

You: So, you're the supervisor for the ADHD rotation. Can you tell me about it?

Better No. 1

You: I have been looking forward to meeting you because I am especially excited about the ADHD rotation. Can you tell me what opportunities interns have on this rotation?

Bad No. 2

You: Do people actually enjoy living in Idaho? Is there anything to do for fun around here?

Better No. 2

You: Living in Idaho would be a new experience for me. Can you tell me what you have enjoyed about this location?

Bad No. 3

You: Do most people get jobs in private practice when they leave this internship?

Better No. 3

You: I am really looking forward to beginning my private practice after internship, and I hear that this site offers good training experiences to help with that. Has that been the experience of most prior interns?

Exhibit 5.2. *Questions to Ask Internship Faculty*

1. What is a typical day like for an intern here?
2. What are you looking for in an intern?
3. What has the impact of managed care been on the program (if applicable)? How has it affected the rotation(s)? Affected the length of stay? Affected the role of the intern?
4. Do you anticipate changes in your program in the next year (rotations, staff)?
5. What is the relationship between psychology and psychiatry departments here? Other disciplines?
6. What do you think the strengths of this internship are?
7. What do interns usually do after internship?
8. Are there opportunities for postdocs here? (Conveys that you are excited about internship and your career; will be applying for postdocs, jobs, and so forth.)
   - What kind of professional guidance is offered?
   - Are they supportive through the postdoc and job-seeking process?
   - Does the internship play an active role in trying to place its graduates?
9. Ask if not explained in materials
   - Seminars and educational opportunities or didactics and typical topics?
   - Intern evaluation process? Quality? Frequency? By whom?
   - Do they strive for breadth or specialty training?
10. Treatment opportunities
    - Individual/group/families/couples/age ranges?
    - Specific populations?
    - Typical referral questions on a specific rotation?
    - Proportion of inpatient and outpatient?
    - Continuity of care? Can you follow the patient from an inpatient stay on an outpatient basis?
    - Inpatient severity of pathology? Length of stay? Role of intern on the unit?
    - How are rotations assigned?
    - How are patients assigned to treatments? Flexibility in assignments?
11. Supervision
    - How are supervisors assigned?
    - Individual/group?
    - Hours per week or case?
    - Live? Video? Audio?
    - How many supervisors does each intern have?
    - Theoretical orientation of supervisors? Which is most strongly represented?
12. Assessment
    - Center's assessment philosophy?
    - Availability?
    - Typical frequency?
    - Emphasis?
    - Neuropsychology?
    - Opportunities outside of rotations?
    - Projectives?
    - Proportion of assessment to therapy?
13. Research
    - How strong of an emphasis do you place on research?
    - What are the opportunities for research?
    - How are research topics selected?
    - What activities might you have the opportunity to become involved with?
    - "I understand you are conducting research in X. Would an incoming intern have the opportunity to work with you in that area?"
14. Resources
    - Computer support?
    - Office?
    - Treatment rooms?
    - Referral agencies?
15. Is there ever a need to travel to other satellite clinics?
16. Are interns ever on call after hours?
17. How are emergencies managed? What is the typical frequency of emergencies?

Exhibit 5.3. *Questions to Ask the Current Interns*

1. Example of a workday/week: Typical activities? Hours per day/week? Meetings? Didactics?
   - Amount of work you take home?
   - What types of assessments?
   - How much time on assessment?
   - How many assessments per week? Write them at work or at home?
2. How is time divided among assessment, treatment, consultation, and psychotherapy?
3. Role of interns at site? With faculty?
4. Relationship between interns and faculty?
   - Do you feel that you are highly regarded by the faculty?
   - Supervision satisfaction?
   - Availability? On site if you encounter a problem?
5. Strengths of the program? Best thing?
6. Limitations/disappointments with the program? Worst thing?
7. Physical resources: Computer? Office space? Treatment rooms? Phone? Beeper?
8. On-call hours?
9. Paperwork?
10. Health care
    - Quality?
    - Satisfactory?
11. Time to work on dissertation?
12. Rotations
    - What rotations are you doing?
    - Most rewarding?
    - Least rewarding?
    - Support among the interns?
    - Number of interns on rotations at a time (one or more than one)?
    - Hours?
    - Supervision?
13. Cost of living?
14. Availability of affordable housing?
15. Do you like the city?
16. Do you socialize with faculty? With other interns?
17. Time for fun?
18. What has your experience at the site been like?
19. What has helped and impeded your adjustment to the site?
20. Where are you from? What program? What type of program?
21. What influenced your decision to select this internship?
22. For you, a year ago, what didn't you ask that would be important to know?

Bad No. 4

You: I hear that there is not much data out there supporting the incremental validity of measures like the Rorschach beyond what one could learn from a good diagnostic interview. How come y'all still administer that measure?

Better No. 4

You: I come from a program that does not emphasize training in projective assessments, but I notice that is a large component of the rotation that you supervise. What is your position on the recent debates regarding evidence-based assessment and treatment?

PURPOSE AND GOALS OF THE INTERVIEW

In the end, the interview provides you with an opportunity to elaborate on your strengths and weaknesses, or in other words, the opportunities that exist for you to be further trained. The interview allows you to further articulate and define your training goals and how the site can help you reach them. The site is assessing how trainable you are for their site. If they are unable to find an area in which they can teach you, then they will consider you a poor fit for their site. Although it may not always seem like it, remember that you are also interviewing the site. After all, you will be making a large investment of time and even money to intern at a particular site. You need to find a site where you will feel comfortable, be able to develop and grow your skills, and fit in. This is an opportunity for you to identify common clinical and research interests and truly become excited about teaming up together for a year. And, sometimes most important, a site wants to learn through the interview that you are likeable, easy to work with, open to feedback, and normal!

THANK-YOU NOTES

Opinions vary about whether or not you should send a thank-you note or other correspondence to follow-up after an interview. Thank-you notes certainly are not required or necessary, and the presence or absence of a note or particular type of note (e.g., e-mail, typed letter, handwritten notecard, hologram delivered by carrier pigeon) will rarely influence the decision of the admissions committee. We suggest that you send a follow-up if it is consistent with your interpersonal style and feels like something you'd like to do. Thank-you notes can be a courteous, appropriate way to express gratitude to your hosts, and therefore the practice is quite common among intern applicants.

In addition to an expression of gratitude, thank-you notes offer a final opportunity to express your interest in the site and explicitly state your perception of the fit between the site and your interests or training goals. Let the note be an extension of your own style and the level of professionalism that you have communicated throughout the application process. Several sample thank-you notes have been included at the end of this chapter as examples, should you wish to send one.

Applicants often face a dilemma when deciding whether to send separate thank-you notes to each person with whom they interviewed at one site or to send a note only to the training director. Again, there is no right or wrong answer. E-mail notes can be easily forwarded to many, but individually typed letters to more than a dozen faculty members at a site may be a bit excessive.

A few suggestions when writing thank-you notes include the following:

- Thank-you notes may demonstrate initiative and genuine interest, and they may help to make you memorable. Keep them simple, and make them personal if you are able.
- Follow-up can be another opportunity to highlight something positive about your CV, experience, training, or interview. Send your note within a day or so after your interview so you will be fresh on the mind of the individual who receives your note.

Sample Thank-You Note 1

January 24, 2008

Dear Dr. X,

I enjoyed meeting with you on January 16, and I am very impressed with your program. Speaking with you, Dr. Y, Dr. Z, and the current interns was helpful to me in forming a more complete understanding of the XXX Consortium.

Overall, I believe that the rotations and experiences offered at XXX match my goals for internship training. Additionally, the pediatric research opportunities are another attractive aspect of your training program.

In addition to the variety of training opportunities, I was greatly impressed by the friendliness and warmth of the people at XXX. I believe that I would be happy and honored to work with everyone with whom I met during my visit.

I am very enthusiastic about my visit to XXX. As per our conversation on January 23, I believe that XXX provides an optimal fit with my previous experiences and future interests for internship training.

Sincerely,

Your Name

Sample Thank-You Note 2

February 1, 2008

Dear Dr. X,

I wanted to thank you for taking the time to meet with me to discuss my internship application and your program. After hearing so many positive things about the internship from friends and colleagues, it was nice to leave the interview day with the same positive feelings myself!

I am very impressed with and excited about the training opportunities your internship has to offer. I feel that your internship's strong adherence to the scientist–practitioner model, with attention devoted to both clinical and research training, is unique among the internship programs I have explored. XXX seems like an ideal place for me to gain breadth in my clinical training, as well as have the opportunity to apply my research skills to areas in pediatric psychology other than studying pediatric pain. Some of the research projects we discussed (e.g., familial transmission in pediatric obesity) were incredibly interesting and exciting to me!

Again, thank you for your time, and I hope that you will consider me for your fine internship.

Sincerely,

Your Name

January 20, 2008

Dear Dr. X,

Thank you for taking the time to meet with me to discuss my internship application and your program. I enjoyed the tour of the hospital and also appreciated hearing about your work; the training opportunities available in the sleep disorders clinic sounded particularly interesting! I am very impressed with your internship program and think that XXX would be an ideal place for me to continue my clinical and research training.

Again, thank you for your time, and I hope that you will continue to consider me for your internship.

Sincerely,

Your Name

Sample Thank-You Note 4

January 30, 2008

Dear Dr. X and Dr. Y,

I appreciated the opportunity to interview with you over the telephone. I was especially struck by the important questions you asked about clinical competency in diversity issues that were embedded in the vignettes posed. Since the telephone interview, I have continued to think about your site, the vignettes, and your brochure. The more I think about the training opportunities at your site, the more excited I become with the thought of being matched to XXX.

I look forward to have the opportunity to meet you in person—I hope by being matched to your site.

Thank you for the invitation to call or write with further questions regarding your internship site. As I learn more about your training philosophy and internship site, I become more and more convinced that XXX would be an ideal match for me.

Sincerely,

Your Name

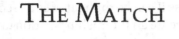

6 THE MATCH

Once your internship interviews have been completed, the next step is to begin thinking about how to navigate the computer Match. The Match was first implemented in 1999 by the Association of Psychology Postdoctoral and Internship Centers (APPIC) to deal with an internship selection process that, frankly, had become a nightmare for applicants. Before then, applicants had to endure pressure tactics, "game playing," and indirect or inappropriate communication by internship sites. Although the Match has not made internship selection stress free, it has made a huge difference in the lives of applicants.

The Match may seem somewhat daunting at first; however, you will find it to be an easy, straightforward, and user-friendly process. This chapter provides an overview of that process, along with tips about how to make the Match work best for you.

THE TWO-PHASE MATCH PROCESS

In 2011, APPIC made some very significant changes to the internship selection process. Previously, applicants who were unplaced during the Match went through a chaotic process known as the "Clearinghouse," in which applicants would apply to programs with unfilled positions as quickly as they could, while sites would interview and make offers to students at an accelerated pace. The Clearinghouse was widely experienced by applicants as chaotic and unfair, and this feedback ultimately led APPIC to try a different approach.

In an attempt to make the process fairer and more organized for unmatched applicants, the Clearinghouse was replaced in 2011 with a second Match ("Phase II"). The original Match is now known as "Phase I" and, as before, includes all applicants and positions and will continue to fill the vast majority of internship positions. Phase II begins immediately upon the conclusion of Phase I and includes applicants who were unmatched in Phase I

DOI: 10.1037/13946-006
Internships in Psychology: The APAGS Workbook for Writing Successful Applications and Finding the Right Fit, Third Edition, by C. Williams-Nickelson, M. J. Prinstein, and W. G. Keilin

and positions that were unfilled in Phase I. Phase II can be thought of as a "second chance" opportunity for students who were unable to secure an internship position during Phase I.

So, each phase is actually its own separate selection process, each with the following steps: (a) application submission, (b) interviews, (c) constructing and submitting a Rank Order List (ROL), and (d) distribution of the Match results.

Timeline

Your participation in the APPIC Match occurs at several distinct times during the internship selection process:

Date	Activity
March 15	Subscribe to the MATCH-NEWS e-mail list.
September–October	Register for the APPIC Match.
Late January–Early February	Construct and submit your ROL for Phase I of the Match.
Late February	Receive your Match results.
March	Phase II of the Match is conducted.

Each of these activities is described in detail in this chapter.

Subscribing to MATCH-NEWS

APPIC sponsors a free e-mail list service, called MATCH-NEWS, that provides valuable information about the Match (along with tips and suggestions about the application process) directly from the APPIC Match Coordinator. American Psychological Association of Graduate Students (APAGS) leaders and staff subscribe to this list to monitor announcements and changes in the process. It is strongly recommended that all applicants subscribe to this list as early as possible in the process (ideally by March 15 of the year in which you intend to apply, though some applicants subscribe a year or two earlier in order to familiarize themselves with the process). MATCH-NEWS is a low-volume list and usually generates no more than five e-mail messages per month.

To subscribe to MATCH-NEWS, first send a blank e-mail to subscribe-match-news@lyris.appic.org. Shortly after sending this e-mail, you should receive a return e-mail requesting that you confirm your subscription. Once you have completed that confirmation process, you should receive a "welcome" message from the list, which indicates that you have successfully subscribed and will receive future messages. Once subscribed, you can review previous messages that were posted to the list by following the instructions in the "E-mail Lists" section of the APPIC website (http://www. appic.org). More information about APPIC's e-mail lists, including a discussion list for applicants called "INTERN-NETWORK," may be found here as well.

MATCH REGISTRATION

The APPIC Match is conducted by National Matching Services, Inc. (NMS), a company located in Toronto, Canada, that specializes in professional matching services. Match registration typically opens in late July or early August. To register for the Match, simply go to the NMS website (http://www.natmatch.com/psychint) and complete the online registration process. The Match registration fee covers your participation in *both* phases of the Match; in other words, if you need to participate in Phase II, you will *not* need to register again, and you will *not* be charged another registration fee. Please note that registering for the Match is an entirely *separate* process from registering for the AAPI Online service.

During the Match registration process, you will be assigned a five-digit applicant code number that uniquely identifies you for the purposes of the Match. You will also be assigned a confidential password/PIN that will allow you to access the important functions on the NMS website, such as submitting your ROL and obtaining your Match result. Keep this password/PIN in a secure place. Once you have registered for the Match, be sure to enter your applicant code number into the designated area of your application within the AAPI Online service.

Although APPIC recommends that applicants register for the Match no later than December 1, it is a good idea to register by mid to late October so that you will receive your applicant code number in time to include it on your AAPI. Remember, though, that the registration fee is nonrefundable and not transferable to another selection year. Thus, if you are unsure about whether you will be participating in the APPIC Match this year (e.g., if you are unsure if you will meet your department's requirements in time, or if you aren't certain that you will be pursuing an internship during this cycle), you might want to wait until later in the process to register, once those uncertainties have been resolved. If you do not register for the Match prior to submitting your internship applications, don't worry—simply enter your applicant code number into the AAPI Online service once you have registered. If you register after December 31, you must obtain the approval of your director of clinical training (DCT).

To have your registration properly processed, it is *very* important that you describe your program accurately when registering. Applicants who are enrolled in doctoral programs that are APPIC "Associates" (i.e., programs that have paid an annual fee to APPIC for special services and discounts for their students) receive a discount on their Match registration fee. The NMS website lists those programs that are APPIC Associates, but you should also check with your DCT to obtain your program's APPIC associate number so that you can ensure that your Match registration is accurate.

APPIC Associate status is by doctoral program, not by department, school, or university; thus, one doctoral program at your university may be an APPIC Associate, whereas another program may not. If your doctoral program is not an APPIC Associate, consider encouraging your faculty members to affiliate with APPIC, as it will reduce the registration cost for you and for other applicants from your program.

For example, let's say you attend Beachcomber University in Miami, Florida, and the NMS website shows the following listing for your university.

Miami	**BEACHCOMBER UNIVERSITY**	
	CLINICAL: Frank A. Johnson, PhD	Associate 801
	COUNSELING: Janet Q. Doe, PhD	Associate 802

In this example, the students in the clinical and counseling psychology programs under DCTs Johnson and Doe at Beachcomber University are entitled to the reduced Match fee because both of those programs are listed as APPIC Associates, with associate numbers 801 and 802, respectively. However, students enrolled in the school psychology program at that same university are not entitled to the discount because their program is not listed as an APPIC Associate.

Once you have completed your registration, you will not need to think much more about the Match until you have finished the interviewing process.

Constructing Your Rank Order List

After the whirlwind of interviewing in December and January comes to a close and you have a chance to evaluate each of your potential internship programs, you will need to determine your order of preference for these programs. Ultimately, you will need to develop an ROL for the Match, which is a list of internship programs to which you have applied in the order in which you prefer them.

One important consideration that we cannot overemphasize is the following: The order in which you rank internship programs should reflect only your true preferences, without regard for how you think these programs have ranked you, whether the programs will be ranking you, or what sort of pressure you might have experienced from others to rank programs. Thus, the program that you are most excited about should be ranked first on your ROL, your next most preferred program should be ranked second, and so forth.

Why is it so important for you to rank programs in the order in which you truly prefer them? The Match algorithm has been specifically designed to allow you to think only about your own needs and preferences, providing an opportunity for you to make ranking decisions in as pressure-free an environment as possible. The computer has been programmed to respect your rankings, and you will be matched to the highest-ranked program on your list that ranks you and does not fill its positions with more-preferred applicants. If you deviate from using your true preferences—for example, by trying to guess how a site has ranked you and adjusting your rankings on the basis of this assumption—you will likely end up hurting yourself because you could end up being matched to a less-preferred program. You will receive the best outcome only if you rank programs in the order in which *you* want to attend them.

Many applicants worry about not being matched, and such concerns can be a significant source of temptation to submit an ROL that doesn't reflect one's true preferences. However, it's important to know that the order of your rankings will affect only *where* you are matched, not *whether* you will be matched. In other words, if the ROL that you submit results in your not being matched, then you can know that the same unfortunate outcome would have occurred if you had submitted an ROL with those same programs ordered differently. Changing the order of your rankings will not increase or decrease your chances of being matched (although, of course, it could affect *where* you get matched). Thus, submitting an ROL that reflects other than your true preferences is a very poor strategy.

Some additional points to remember about constructing your ROL:

- You may rank as many programs as you wish.
- Your rankings remain confidential. Internship programs will never be told where you have ranked them, either before or after the Match.
- In general, you should rank all of the programs at which you are being considered. However, you should omit any program from your list that you consider unacceptable. In other words, if you do not want to be matched to a particular program under any circumstances, simply omit that program from your ROL. You cannot be matched to any program that is not listed on your ROL.

- You should remember that the results of the Match are binding, which means that you are required to attend the internship program to which you are matched. And, although most applicants are matched to one of their highly ranked programs, it is possible for you to be matched to any program that is included on your ROL. So, again, do not include a program on your ROL if you do not want to be matched to that program.
- Each program in the Match has a six-digit "program code number" that must be used when constructing your rankings. A list of participating programs and their program code numbers is available on the NMS website after November 1 of each year.
- Some internship sites may have more than one program code number, usually to represent different rotations or training experiences. For example, a site with a neuropsychology rotation and a geropsychology rotation may use a different program code number for each, allowing you to rank the programs separately on your ROL. Sites should clarify for you (in their written materials or during the interview process) how their program code numbers are affiliated with which programs, rotations, or training experiences.

To better illustrate the ranking process, let's say that you have applied to several internship programs, and your true preferences for these programs dictate that you rank them in the following order:

Your True Preferences

999901—Really Fine Community Mental Health Center
888801—Better Health Hospital: Neuropsychology Program
777701—Truly Wonderful Medical Center
888802—Better Health Hospital: Geropsychology Program
666601—Sunshine Hospital

In this illustration, you have decided to rank two separate programs at the Better Health Hospital using each program's unique program code number. Because you prefer the neuropsychology program over the geropsychology program, these rankings reflect this preference.

Let's throw some twists into this scenario with a couple of examples.

Example 1. Let's say that the Sunshine Hospital calls you and tells you that you are a truly wonderful applicant and offers you free housing and a boat to use during your internship year. In fact, they violate Match policies and tell you that they are ranking you as their number one choice.

Question: Given this situation, should you move Sunshine Hospital higher on your ROL so you don't "miss out" on them?

Answer: Absolutely not. Because your true preference is for Sunshine Hospital to be ranked fifth, the best and only approach is to leave them ranked fifth. If Sunshine Hospital does rank you as their number one choice, you will definitely be matched to them only if the computer is unable to match you to the four higher-ranked programs on your list. In other words, you haven't reduced your chances of getting matched to Sunshine Hospital by ranking your more-preferred programs higher on your list.

Example 2. Let's say that the Really Fine Community Mental Health Center (CMHC) doesn't seem that interested in you. In fact, even though you got a highly favorable impression of the program during your interview, you suspect that you did a horrible job in responding to their interview questions. Despite this interview fiasco, they remain your most preferred site.

> *Question:* Given this situation, should you move Really Fine CMHC lower on your list based on your assumption that they aren't going to rank you very highly?

> *Answer:* Absolutely not; you should definitely rank Really Fine CMHC as number one on your list.

If the computer is not successful in matching you to Really Fine CMHC, it will simply go to the next site on your list without having penalized you in any way. In other words, by ranking the Really Fine CMHC as number one, you have not reduced your chances of being matched to any other site on your list. Thus, you don't get penalized for ranking sites that you consider to be long shots.

Submitting Your Rank Order List

Once you have constructed your ROL, you must then log in to the NMS website (http://www.natmatch.com/psychint) and use the Rank Order List Input and Confirmation (ROLIC) system to submit your rankings to the Match. To log in to the ROLIC system, use your applicant code number and the password/PIN that was previously provided to you by NMS. Entering your rankings via the ROLIC system is a simple and straightforward process, and complete instructions are available on the NMS website. Once you have finished entering your ROL, you must certify it, which designates your list as being complete and ready to use in the Match.

If you change your mind about your rankings before the submission deadline, you can log in again to the ROLIC system and make the appropriate changes to your ROL. You can do this even if your list was previously certified (but be sure to recertify the list once you have made your changes). Here's a tip: Don't wait until the last day to enter your rankings! You don't want to risk being unable to access the ROLIC system if you encounter Internet connection problems or a busy server.

Every registered applicant must submit either an ROL or a formal withdrawal from the Match. If you do not have any programs to rank (e.g., you had the disappointing experience of not receiving any interviews, or your situation changed and you decided not to participate in the Match), then you *must* submit a withdrawal from the Match. This lets NMS know that you will not be participating in Phase I. Even if you withdraw from Phase I of the Match, you may still choose to participate in Phase II and/or the Post-Match Vacancy Service.

Receiving Your Match Result

Once you have submitted your ROL for Phase I, there is nothing left to do but wait for the Match processing to take place. The wait between the ROL submission deadline and the release of the Match results is just over 2 weeks. Although the wait can be excruciating, this time period is absolutely necessary for NMS to ensure that the Match is conducted accurately. While you wait, NMS extensively checks and rechecks the Match processing to ensure that all applicants and programs receive the best possible match.

The release of the Match results for Phase I occurs in late February—generally on a Friday at 10:00 a.m. EST (be sure to adjust this time to your own time zone)—on a day known as "APPIC Phase I Match Day." On this day, you will learn whether or not you were successfully matched to an internship program and, if so, the name of the program to which you were matched. In addition, on this day, internship programs are told the names of the applicants to whom they have been matched. For applicants who do not receive a match, the second phase of the Match (described below) begins operating on this day.

There are three ways to obtain your Match results:

- *Via e-mail:* NMS will attempt to send you an e-mail message no later than 10:00 a.m. Eastern Time on Match Day. In fact, NMS actually begins sending result information via e-mail an hour or two before the official 10:00 a.m. Eastern Time release time. Thus, your result e-mail may actually arrive a bit earlier than 10:00 a.m. Eastern Time on Match Day. Keep in mind that e-mail is subject to delays or errors and thus is not 100% reliable (in fact, an estimated 5% of applicants do not receive this e-mail in a timely fashion). If you do not receive this e-mail, check your spam or junk mail folder. If that doesn't work, you may use one of the two additional methods to obtain your Match results:
- *Via the Internet:* Beginning at 10:00 a.m. Eastern Time on Match Day, you may use your applicant code number and password/PIN to log in to the NMS website to obtain your results.
- *Via your DCT:* If you are enrolled in an APPIC Associate doctoral program, your DCT will have access to your Match results.

On Match Day, after you have received the name of the site to which you have been matched, there is one additional detail to take care of: talk with your new training director! Most training directors like to talk with their new interns on this day to provide a personal welcome. Training directors and applicants are allowed to contact each other after 11:00 a.m. Eastern Time on Match Day, and training directors usually, but not always, initiate calls to their new interns after that time. You may recall that you provided a telephone number on your application where you can be reached between 11:00 a.m. and 1:00 p.m. Eastern Time on that day, and it's best to remain available at that number during that time. If you do not receive a call from your new training director during that period, it is possible that he or she is having difficulty reaching you, and you should call him or her to acknowledge the Match result.

Finally, training directors are required to send you a written appointment agreement, postmarked or e-mailed no later than 7 days after Match Day. If you have not received this agreement within 2 weeks after Match Day, contact your new training director to inquire about its status.

Without a doubt, learning that you did not get matched to an internship site is the most painful and challenging outcome of the application process. And with the increasing imbalance between the number of applicants and the number of available positions, it is a situation that more and more students are finding themselves in each year. APPIC provides two services for unmatched students to find an internship position: Phase II of the APPIC Match and the APPIC Post-Match Vacancy Service. These steps are described later in this chapter.

APPIC Match Policies

APPIC has developed a set of policies that guide the operation of the Match. These policies are available for viewing or downloading on both the APPIC and NMS websites and are included with the registration instructions that you received from NMS. It is imperative that you read these policies carefully early in the process, and in particular before your interviews, as you are expected to abide by them throughout the selection process. APPIC does take action against internship programs and applicants who violate the policies.

Although not a substitute for actually reading the Match policies, here are some of the more important considerations for internship applicants.

First, applicants and programs are not permitted to communicate, solicit, accept, or use any ranking-related information before the release of the Match results. Furthermore, applicants and programs may never ask about how they have been ranked, even after the release of the Match results. Some examples of what applicants should *never* say to an internship program include the following:

- "You are my first choice."
- "You are one of my top-ranked sites."
- "I really like your site better than the other sites at which I've interviewed."
- "Where do you intend to rank me?"

Even with these restrictions, it is important to understand that the policies are not intended to restrict the expression of genuine interest or enthusiasm about a program. So, here are some examples of what is permissible:

- "I have really enjoyed my interview with you today."
- "I am very impressed with your internship program."
- "I really like this neuropsychology rotation, and I really believe that it will meet my training needs."
- "Your internship faculty seem to be very invested in the training needs of your interns."
- "After visiting your inpatient program, I don't think it is quite what I'm looking for. However, I would still very much like to be considered for your outpatient program, as that seems to be a much better fit for me."

So, the best approach is to simply follow the normal guidelines of courteous and professional communication while not making any statements about rankings or about comparing one internship program with another.

Second, each internship program that conducts onsite or telephone interviews must notify you as to whether you will be interviewed, no later than the interview notification date listed for that program in the *APPIC Directory*.

Third, the results of the Match are binding. Once you submit an ROL to the Match, you are obligated to attend the internship program to which you are matched. Similarly, the program to which you are matched is required to accept you as an intern for the coming year.

Fourth, after the Match is completed, training directors are required to send you a written appointment agreement outlining the conditions of the appointment, such as stipend, fringe benefits, and the beginning and ending dates of the internship year.

Couples

The APPIC Match has special procedures to assist applicants who are members of a couple when both partners are applying for psychology internships in the same year. These procedures allow a couple to maximize their chances of being located in the same geographic area. Although couples are not required to use these procedures, virtually all couples find it advantageous to do so. More information about this option is available at both the APPIC and NMS websites.

Resolving Problems

APPIC has developed two programs to assist applicants who are experiencing difficulties with the selection process or their internship experience:

- *Informal Problem Consultation:* This process allows you to consult confidentially with an APPIC representative to discuss your concerns and to identify options and solutions. If desired, APPIC may become directly involved in negotiating a resolution among parties. Over the past few years, APPIC has found this process to be a highly effective way of resolving difficulties experienced by applicants.
- *Formal Complaints:* APPIC also has a formal complaint process and has established the APPIC Standards and Review Committee to handle such complaints. In response to a formal complaint, the APPIC board may impose sanctions on programs or applicants who violate APPIC policies.

Staying Informed

Several resources are available that provide additional information about the Match, answer your questions, and generally keep you informed about the process.

- Extensive information is available at the APPIC and NMS websites (http://www.natmatch.com/psychint and http://www.appic.org).
- Be sure that you subscribe to the MATCH-NEWS list, as described earlier in this chapter, as early as possible in the process.
- APPIC also maintains an e-mail discussion list, INTERN-NETWORK, that allows current and former intern applicants, training directors, APPIC board

members, and APAGS representatives to discuss various aspects of the selection process. This is a popular place for internship applicants to get answers to their questions about the AAPI, interviews, the Match, or any other aspect of the process. To subscribe, simply send a blank e-mail message to subscribe-intern-network@lyris.appic.org. Because this list can generate a lot of e-mail in busy times, you may wish to set your subscription to "digest" mode, which allows you to receive a maximum of one e-mail per day that contains all of the messages that were posted to the list in the preceding 24 hours. To sign up for digest mode, first subscribe as already described, and then send a blank e-mail to digest-intern-network@lyris.appic.org.

- The APPIC Match coordinator, Dr. Greg Keilin, is always happy to answer your questions or assist you with the process. He may be contacted at gkeilin@mail.utexas.edu or (512) 475-6949.

PHASE II OF THE MATCH

So, it is the Friday in late February known as "Phase I Match Day," and you have just received that dreaded e-mail message that says, "We regret to inform you that you did not match to a position." Now what?

First and foremost, if you find yourself without a match, this is not the time to be questioning yourself, your competencies, or your suitability for the profession of psychology (even though those are normal reactions to this frustrating turn of events). It is also not the time to isolate yourself or to get stuck in your disappointment, embarrassment, anger, fear, confusion, hopelessness, or any of the myriad of emotions that you may be experiencing. Instead, talk with family, friends, fellow graduate students, and trusted faculty members about the situation and your feelings. By mobilizing your support systems, along with your energies, resources, and creativity, you will be well prepared to move forward with the next step of the process.

The fact of the matter is that unmatched applicants are typically highly competent and talented individuals. How do we know this? Because internship training directors routinely tell us that some of their best interns have been students who were unmatched during Phase I but were later placed at their site (e.g., during Phase II). In addition, there are now literally thousands of "ex–unmatched applicants" who ultimately found an internship and are now happy and settled as licensed, practicing psychologists.

Each year, there are about 300 positions that are not filled in Phase I of the APPIC Match. Phase II of the Match is an opportunity for unmatched applicants to apply for these unfilled positions. It is, quite simply, a second application and matching process that occurs in an accelerated fashion. Phase II lasts about a month (late February to late March) from start to finish, and it includes (a) a period for students to submit applications to sites, (b) a period for interviews to be conducted, (c) the submission of new ROLs, and (d) the distribution of Phase II Match results. There are no additional Match or AAPI Online fees in order to participate in Phase II.

If you registered for the Match during Phase I and did not get matched to an internship position during Phase I, then you are eligible to participate in Phase II. This is true even if you withdrew or didn't submit an ROL during Phase I. However, you must have registered during Phase I in order to be eligible for Phase II, as new Match registrations are not permitted during Phase II.

While this section provides you with an overview of how Phase II works, complete instructions, along with a set of Frequently Asked Questions, can be found on the APPIC (http://www.appic.org) and NMS (http://www.natmatch.com/psychint) websites.

Step 1: Preparation

First, review the timeline for Phase II. You will notice that Phase II begins at 11:00 a.m. Eastern Time on Phase I Match Day and that you have 6 days (as of this writing) to decide where to apply during Phase II and to submit your applications. While you will likely find the 6-day period to be a sufficient amount of time to get that done, it also means that you need to begin moving forward as soon as possible. Thus, you will likely want to clear your schedule for several days, giving you the time to focus on this next step of the process.

The good news about this accelerated timeline is that internship training directors will not be able to view any Phase II applications until the end of the 6-day application period. This allows you to move through these steps in a measured way, without the pressure of having to submit your application before others do.

It is vitally important at this stage to clarify for yourself the types of internships you are willing to consider in this next phase of the process. For example, given that accredited internship positions will be considerably harder to find in Phase II, are you willing to consider unaccredited internships? What about non-APPIC member internships? (If you consider unaccredited and/or non-APPIC internships, be sure that you understand the implications of such a decision; see Chapter 1, "Getting Started," for specifics.) Are you willing to broaden your internship search to different settings, populations, training opportunities, and so on? Where might you be willing to relocate? What is the minimum level of funding you would accept? Which of these options will be supported by your doctoral program? Thinking about these issues now, and in particular consulting with your DCT and other faculty, will help you decide where to apply in Phase II.

Be sure to carefully review the information about Phase II on the APPIC website, including the Phase II "Getting Started" guide for applicants and the Frequently Asked Questions. Those pages contain comprehensive and specific information about how to navigate Phase II as well as feedback from previous unmatched applicants about how to make the most of the process.

Step 2: Review the List of Available Positions

Once Phase II of the Match begins, a list of programs with available positions is posted on the NMS website (http://www.natmatch.com/psychint). This list consists primarily of positions that were unfilled from Phase I of the Match, along with a few additional positions that may have come open too late to be included in Phase I (perhaps, e.g., because of funding delays).

The list is organized by state or province, and then by city, and contains basic information about each program along with a link to the site's *APPIC Directory Online* listing (for sites that are APPIC members). The list is not updated once it is released, and each entry looks something like this:

BLOOMING DAISIES MENTAL HEALTH CENTER

1234 MAIN STREET
DIAGNOSIS, NEW MEXICO 12345
Telephone: (222) 222-2222
E-mail: Jane.Smith@BloomingDaisiesMHC.org
Director: Jane Smith, PhD
APPIC Member: Yes (Link to APPIC Directory Listing)
Accreditation: APA—NO CPA—NO
Program: Pediatrics
Code: 999901 Openings: 1
Program: Neuropsychology
Code: 999902 Openings: 2

In addition to this list, APPIC sponsors a "late-breaking news" service during Phase II that allows internship training directors to post news or updates about their available positions. For example, a program may want to publicize special application requirements for the available position(s) or revise its selection criteria, or simply provide additional information about its vacancy(ies). These late-breaking items are available on a special page of the APPIC website, which is updated frequently as new information is received from programs. APPIC recommends that you wait until the first set of news items is posted (usually the day after Phase II begins) before submitting any applications.

When deciding where to apply, it is usually best to apply to sites that are a good fit with your interests and background. Taking a shotgun approach (i.e., applying to a large number of sites without regard for how qualified you are for those positions) is generally a poor strategy, and your time is likely better spent on carefully selecting programs that are a good fit for you and writing thoughtful cover letters. Training directors often complain that they receive many applications during Phase II from students who are clearly not qualified and/or who are poor fits for their programs, and such applications are rarely successful.

Students often wonder, during Phase II, if it is acceptable to apply to programs to which they previously applied (e.g., during Phase I). Yes, absolutely. In fact, some programs may actually prefer applicants who previously applied, even if those applicants weren't initially successful in getting an interview or being matched to that program.

Step 3: Preparing Your Applications

You will use the AAPI Online service to submit your applications in Phase II, just as you did in Phase I. In fact, the application that you used in Phase I will remain available to you during Phase II. While the "core" part of your application remains locked and unchangeable, you may use the same CV(s), essays, and letters of recommendation, or you may submit new ones. As noted below, you will need to write a new cover letter for each program to which you apply in Phase II. Your graduate transcripts remain on file and thus do not need to be resubmitted.

One thing to consider is whether you should take the time to revise your essays, take a different approach in your cover letters, update your CV, etc. This is a decision that should be made in consultation with your faculty, although you should remember that changes must be completed within the 6-day application submission window. It is also acceptable to ask for feedback from training directors at sites to which you submitted applications during Phase I, although getting such feedback soon enough to use to apply in Phase II can be challenging. In deciding whether to make such revisions, consider how well your applications were received during Phase I; if you received relatively few or no offers of interviews, then a revision of your application materials may be in order.

As of this writing, APPIC strongly recommends that you tailor your cover letters to each site to which you are applying, just as you (we hope) did in Phase I. (You may have heard that it was acceptable to send "generic" cover letters in Phase II, but APPIC changed this approach in 2012.) Thus, in Phase II, your cover letters should describe how you fit with the program and how your interests, experiences, and background are congruent with what the program has to offer.

Please note that you should *not* submit any supplemental materials (e.g., undergraduate transcripts, testing reports) to sites even if a site's application instructions tell you to do so. Training directors understand this limitation and will not expect your application in Phase II to include supplemental materials. Later in the process, sites may contact selected applicants from their pool and ask them to provide additional information; if you receive such a request, you will need to provide that information separately from the AAPI Online service, such as via e-mail.

Step 4: Submitting Your Applications

APPIC has established an application deadline, which is currently 6 days after Phase II of the Match begins. As previously mentioned, internship training directors will not be able to see or review any submitted applications until this deadline date. Although training directors may choose to continue receiving applications after the deadline, most will choose to shut off the submission of applications at that time. Thus, you should be sure to have all of your applications submitted within the 6-day window.

To submit an application, simply follow the same steps that you used to submit an application during Phase I. You will be permitted to submit applications only to those programs that are participating in Phase II, and you won't be charged any submission fees by the AAPI Online service.

Step 5: Interviewing

Once the 6-day application phase is completed, the next two-and-a-half weeks involve application review and interviews by programs. Waiting to hear from sites can be challenging during this time, as the amount of time it takes to review applications will vary among sites. Sites often receive dozens, if not hundreds, of applications during Phase II, and thus most are not able to acknowledge receiving applicants' materials or to notify those applicants who do not receive an interview. Although this lack of individual response may seem rude or discourteous, keep in mind that sites are typically overwhelmed by the number of applications that they receive during this time.

One way to use this time is to sharpen your interviewing skills—something that may be particularly relevant if you were offered a significant number of interviews during Phase I but didn't get matched. It is important to remember that the skills that make you a strong graduate student are actually *different* from the skills required to be a strong interviewee. Thus, you can be a terrific clinician, researcher, teacher, etc., but not be as skilled in communicating those strengths during an interview. Role plays with faculty members or others can be a terrific way to get feedback and potentially strengthen your interviewing performance during Phase II.

Receiving an invitation for an interview is typically a sign that the program is seriously considering you, as sites typically conduct a relatively limited number of interviews during Phase II. Because time is limited, most programs offer applicants telephone rather than in-person interviews. However, sites that are local to you may request that you visit them in person.

Step 6: Submitting Your Rank Order List

Once you have completed interviewing, you need to submit your ROL via the NMS website. This step is essentially identical to the submission process that occurred in Phase I. The advice provided earlier in this chapter about ranking programs in the order that you prefer them is just as important in Phase II.

In the unfortunate event that you did not receive any interview offers in Phase II and thus have no programs to rank, you should submit a formal withdrawal from Phase II.

Step 7: Receiving Your Phase II Match Result

The Phase II Match results are distributed in the exact same way as were the Phase I results. If you learn that you matched, congratulations! As in Phase I, your new training director will likely call you to acknowledge the Match results. In addition, she or he is required to send you a written appointment agreement within a week of the conclusion of Phase II.

THE APPIC POST-MATCH VACANCY SERVICE

If you don't get matched in Phase II, there is still another option: the APPIC Post-Match Vacancy Service (PMVS). This service begins operation immediately upon the conclusion of Phase II (usually in late March) and continues throughout the summer and into the fall (currently through October 31). In addition to using the PMVS to post the relative few unfilled positions from Phase II, training directors can also post new positions that are usually created on receipt of additional funding. Applicants do not pay a fee to use the PMVS.

In 2012, 25 internship programs (including 16 APPIC-member programs and four accredited programs) posted one or more positions in the PMVS. While that's not a large number, it is nevertheless worth your attention because there is always the possibility that one or more positions will be posted that fit what you are seeking.

The PMVS is a much less structured process than Phases I and II, as it does not use the AAPI Online service or the APPIC Match and thus looks much more like a typical job application process. In a nutshell, the process looks like this:

(a) Applicants regularly review the current list of available positions on the APPIC website;
(b) when an applicant wishes to apply for a position, she or he submits a cover letter and CV to the program via e-mail;
(c) the site training director reviews applications and conducts interviews; and
(d) when the program has found a suitable candidate, an offer of an internship position is made to the applicant.

Information about participating in the PMVS is provided below. Be sure to consult the APPIC website for more specific instructions as well as any changes to the procedure that may have occurred after the publication of this workbook.

Locating Vacant Positions

In the PMVS, vacancies are posted on a designated page of the APPIC website, in chronological order. APPIC also provides a special e-mail service that, once you are subscribed, will notify you via e-mail whenever that page is updated. Instructions for subscribing to this service are located on the APPIC website.

Preparing and Submitting Your Application

Since the AAPI Online service is *not* used for the PMVS, an alternate application procedure was developed. This procedure limits the amount of information that you may initially submit to an internship program to a cover letter and CV (unless a program specifically requests otherwise). The purpose of this limitation is to prevent training directors' e-mail inboxes from filling up with application materials, as well as to simplify the initial review process for programs. Once they review your cover letter and vita, training directors will contact you if they wish for you to send additional information.

So, you should create a single document in your word processing program that includes both a cover letter and your CV. As previously noted, it is generally best to tailor your cover letter to the site rather than to send a generic version. Use your name as the document name (e.g., "Smith.doc" or "MarySmith.doc") and ensure that the document is readable by Microsoft Word (i.e., with the .doc or .docx suffix). Be sure to include your contact information in this document as well.

When you see a position that interests you, you may simply submit an e-mail to the submission address listed in the announcement. The subject line of the e-mail should include your name (e.g., "Application: Mary Smith") and you should include the document that contains your cover letter and CV as an attachment to the e-mail.

Programs that respond positively to this initial application may request other application materials from you. You should be prepared to submit the following items upon request:

- A formatted copy of your AAPI Online application. This may be downloaded from the Applicant Portal of the AAPI Online service. Be sure to download the nicely formatted PDF version of your application, and to do so before the AAPI Online service closes for the year. This version is very similar to the version that was originally viewed by sites, but it does not include the items that were specific to each site or confidential (e.g., cover letter, CV, essays, letters of reference, transcripts, and your DCT's verification of internship readiness).
- Letters of recommendation and your DCT's verification of internship readiness. Talk with your DCT and letter writers to see what they prefer in terms of getting this information to sites. Some may provide you with copies, while others will prefer to send the information to sites directly upon request.
- Answers to the four essay questions on your application.
- A copy of your transcripts (usually scanned into PDF format).

INTERVIEWS A program that is interested in you will contact you to arrange an interview. Typically, these interviews are scheduled for a specific date or time, but it's also possible that a program may request that you interview "on the spot"—that is, while they have you on the phone. On rare occasions, a site may want you to come for an on-site interview, and it is up to you as to whether or not you want to devote the time and incur the expense of such travel.

RECEIVING AN OFFER A site that wants to offer you a position will generally do so via telephone. In fact, some applicants receive an offer at the conclusion of their telephone interview! Be sure that you are clear about all terms of employment (e.g., salary, benefits, duties of the position) before accepting an offer. The training director is required by APPIC policies to send you an employment agreement, postmarked within 1 week of your acceptance.

Remember, once an offer has been made by a program and accepted by you, it is binding and cannot be changed by either party. Thus, if you accept an offer and are later contacted by a more-preferred site, you cannot renege on your agreement with the original site.

WHAT IF I DO NOT FIND A POSITION? If your efforts to find a position after the Match do not work out, then it is important to take some time to reflect on the process and identify what aspects of your application and/or interview might be improved. Some specific suggestions:

- Consider contacting training directors at sites where you applied during the original Match process in order to request candid feedback about your application and/or interview. Although not all training directors will be willing to provide you such feedback, some will be happy to do so.
- Review the choices that you made during your application process. Did you apply to sites that were all highly competitive? Did you apply to a limited geographic area? Did you apply to sites that may not have been good fits for your interests and/or experiences? Any of these approaches could have had a significant negative impact on your ability to be matched.
- Review your application materials and get feedback from several trusted faculty members about how they can be improved. Were your essays as compelling as they could be? Was there anything in your cover letter or essays that may have come across in a way other than you attended? Did any of your recommenders write a weak letter? Did you have sufficient practicum hours and experiences to be competitive?
- Work on improving your interviewing skills, for example, through mock interviews or a similar process.

7 FREQUENTLY ASKED QUESTIONS FROM PROSPECTIVE INTERNS

This workbook was originally written as a resource to accompany an internship workshop conducted yearly at the American Psychological Association (APA) annual convention. At each workshop, prospective interns asked excellent questions about each aspect of the internship application and selection process. The questions posed and addressed in this chapter are representative of those asked at past workshops and of queries submitted to Association of Psychology Postdoctoral and Internship Centers (APPIC) and American Psychological Association of Graduate Students (APAGS) representatives during the application and selection period.

These questions are distributed across the various sections addressing the specific application tasks. The answers are composite responses that the authors of this workbook consider good advice. As you would with any advice, you should consider these comments along with your own good judgment and the feedback you have received from your director of clinical training.

GETTING STARTED **Question 1. How important is it for me to attend an APA-accredited or APPIC-member internship program?**

First, it is important to mention that there are excellent internship programs that are accredited and/or APPIC members, as well as excellent programs that are neither accredited nor APPIC members. In fact, many students attend nonaccredited and non–APPIC-member programs each year and encounter no problems in their future licensing and employment activities.

However, some students who attend nonaccredited or non–APPIC-member programs do encounter substantial difficulties with the quality of their training, their ability

DOI: 10.1037/13946-007
Internships in Psychology: The APAGS Workbook for Writing Successful Applications and Finding the Right Fit, Third Edition, by C. Williams-Nickelson, M. J. Prinstein, and W. G. Keilin

to get licensed as psychologists, and/or their ability to secure suitable employment. Some states now *require* an accredited internship for licensure. Thus, it is important to understand that there can be potential risks in attending one of these programs.

When considering internship programs, students need to be aware of the requirements of three entities: (a) their doctoral programs, (b) future licensing boards, and (c) future employers.

- *Regarding your doctoral program:* Many doctoral programs require an accredited internship in order to meet graduation requirements. It is important to check with your director of clinical training (DCT) to be sure that you understand what your program requires.
- *Regarding licensing:* Although many students each year complete nonaccredited internships and experience few, if any, difficulties when applying for licensure, you should be aware of the potential risks associated with nonaccredited internships. A few states may require an APA-accredited internship and/or doctoral program to qualify for licensure. Some licensing boards may require additional documentation, or in some cases, additional coursework, for applicants without an accredited internship. For example, at the time of this writing, the Texas State Board of Examiners of Psychologists requires either an APA-accredited internship or an internship that meets a list of specific requirements as defined by that board. Thus, people attempting to get licensed in Texas who attended a non–APA-accredited internship must demonstrate that their internship meets those requirements; if it does not, then that individual could not be licensed in Texas. This issue can get especially tricky if you do not know the specific state in which you intend to practice and thus cannot anticipate the future requirements that you will need to meet. The website of the Association of State and Provincial Psychology Boards (http://www.asppb.org) can be helpful in learning about licensure and in locating information about the requirements of various states.
- *Regarding future employers:* Some employers, such as Veterans Affairs facilities, require the completion of an APA-accredited internship and doctoral program in order to qualify for employment as a psychologist. Other employers may not have such a strict requirement, although some job and postdoc announcements will specify that an APA-accredited internship is a preferred qualification. Again, because it is difficult to know what your future career plans may be, it is advisable to check with your DCT and as many potential employers as possible in order to make an educated decision.

In general, there is no "right" answer as to whether one should consider attending a nonaccredited and/or non–APPIC-member internship program. Attending an accredited program is certainly the safest option, as you almost certainly will not have to justify the quality of your internship to anyone in the future. In addition, it provides you, in effect, with a seal of approval with regard to the quality of training that you will receive and makes it unlikely that your internship program will be a barrier to licensure and/or future employment. Attending an APPIC-member internship that is not accredited does increase the risk to some extent, particularly for licensure boards or employers that require an accredited internship, though most APPIC-member training directors will tell you that their students do just fine overall. Attending a nonaccredited, non–

APPIC-member internship incurs the most risk, given that there has been no external body that has reviewed the site to ensure that it meets established standards of quality and given the potential risks to future licensure and employment opportunities.

The decision as to whether to attend a nonaccredited or non–APPIC-member internship program can be a difficult one, particularly if you are geographically restricted or are attempting to find an internship via the Phase II of the Match or the Post-Match Vacancy Service. We encourage you to consult with faculty or other knowledgeable individuals, to carefully consider your career interests and options, and to familiarize yourself with issues related to licensure and future employment.

Question 2. What if I learn that an internship program is planning to apply, or is in the process of applying, for APPIC membership and/or APA/CPA accreditation?

A site may have the best of intentions, but you should be aware that the application and/or approval processes for initial accreditation and/or APPIC membership could take far longer (even months or years longer) than a program anticipates. There is no guarantee that a program will ultimately attain accreditation and/or APPIC membership or will do so in a timely manner. Thus, although a program's training staff may convey confidence that they will ultimately be successful in the application process, such confidence may or may not be warranted, and you should consider attending such a program only if you clearly understand the risks in doing so.

Question 3. Is it possible to create my own internship site (e.g., by approaching an agency that doesn't have an established internship program and asking them to hire me for a year as an "intern")?

In answering this question, it is important to state that the predoctoral internship year is considered to be far more than simply a year of "work experience." For example, APPIC's current membership criteria state that a psychology internship "is an organized training program which, in contrast to supervised experience or on-the-job training, is designed to provide the intern with a planned, programmed sequence of training experiences." APA and many licensing boards have similar expectations for the internship experience. Creating one's own "internship" almost never meets, or even comes close to, the standards and expectations of these organizations.

So, although it is possible to create your own internship, doing so can jeopardize the quality of the training that you will receive, and (as discussed earlier) carries substantial risks with respect to future licensing and employment opportunities. It is also something that most doctoral programs would not permit. We generally do not recommend this approach unless you are certain that it will be acceptable to your doctoral program, licensing board, and future employers.

Question 4. If I get placed at a nonaccredited internship program, is it acceptable for me to apply for and attend an accredited internship in the future? In other words, is it acceptable to attend two internships?

Although there are no specific rules prohibiting the completion of a second internship, this is truly a bad idea. A nonaccredited internship should not be used as an opportunity to gain additional experience in order to qualify for an accredited internship. Also, once you have attended an internship, it is highly unlikely that another program would be willing to accept you for a second internship, particularly when there are many applicants who have difficulty securing their first internship. You should keep the following points in mind:

- If you are looking to gain additional experience to make yourself a more attractive applicant to accredited internship programs, then you should complete additional practica rather than a nonaccredited internship.
- Give very careful consideration to whether or not you want to attend an accredited internship. If you decide that you definitely want to attend an accredited internship, then you should not apply to or rank any nonaccredited programs, as doing so could result in your being placed at a nonaccredited program.
- A small number of doctoral programs will allow their students to graduate without an internship, and students in these programs sometimes pursue this option with the intent of completing an internship in the future. However, these students may not realize that the internship is designed to be "predoctoral" in nature, meaning that it should be completed while the student is matriculating through her or his doctoral program. As such, APPIC policies require a student to be enrolled in a doctoral program to be eligible for participation in the Match, and students who graduate before completing their internships may lose their eligibility to participate in future APPIC Matches.

Question 5. What are some ways for me to learn about the selection process and the APPIC Match?

We recommend that students begin learning about the selection process and APPIC Match as early in the process as possible. In particular, students should review the information located at two websites: APPIC (http://www.appic.org) and National Matching Services (NMS; http://www.natmatch.com/psychint).

In addition, all applicants should subscribe to the APPIC e-mail list MATCH-NEWS that provides news and information about the Match directly from APPIC. MATCH-NEWS is a low-volume list, which means that you will typically receive only a few e-mail messages per month. A second APPIC e-mail list, INTERN-NETWORK, is a discussion list on which current and former intern applicants, some internship training directors, and APPIC board members discuss various aspects of the selection process.

All applicants are strongly encouraged to subscribe to MATCH-NEWS early in the process; participation in the INTERN-NETWORK discussion list is optional.

Question 6. I have some fairly specialized interests and am looking for an internship that will meet these needs. How do I find such an internship?

First, check the *APPIC Directory Online* to see if the existing search options will allow you to locate an internship that meets your needs. If not, consider submitting an inquiry to the INTERN-NETWORK e-mail list to see if anyone can point you in the right direction. You also might try locating psychologists who are practicing in your area of interest (e.g., through professional organizations or e-mail lists) to see if they have any ideas about internship programs that specialize in this area.

Question 7. I carefully recorded my clinical hours over the past several years, but now I realize that I neglected to document the specifics about one of my brief training experiences. How do I go about estimating my hours?

Documentation of clinical experience typically requires students to report two kinds of information: (a) data about the actual hours spent in professional practice activities and (b) data on the personal characteristics of the clients served in those professional activities. Estimating the data about contact hours may be a simple process if you have a good idea of the number of clients you saw each week. From that bit of data you can extrapolate and generate a good estimate of contact hours over the course of a training experience. Because professionals develop "habits of practice," a proportion of indirect clinical contact to direct contact more than likely is consistent across training experiences. Hence, if you completed 3 hours of indirect service for every 1 hour of direct service in other experiences, chances are good that you engaged in the same kind of clinical balance in this brief training experience.

Estimating the personal characteristics of clientele is more challenging. Referencing the general client data from your training site may be of help. Many sites collect aggregate service data for each month of each year; these data may help remind you about clients you served during that training period. Although it is possible to estimate these important bits of data, no amount of post-experience research or guessing will replace good record-keeping during your training.

Most important, because your DCT is required to sign off on your practicum hours, it is important to discuss with him or her your methods of calculating your hours to ensure that they meet with the DCT's approval.

Question 8. I've had some unique experiences and am confused about how to document them on the APPIC Application for Psychology Internships (AAPI). How do I determine where on the AAPI they should be placed? Similarly, can I include my relevant work experience during my graduate program in my practicum hours?

The first step is to carefully read the instructions that are included with the AAPI, as this is where APPIC has addressed many of the most frequently asked questions about the application.

In general, keep the following points in mind when attempting to document your hours:

- If an experience appears to fall in more than one AAPI category, or does not quite fit into any AAPI category, just use your best judgment to select the category that best captures the experience. Do not obsess or worry about it; there is often not a "right" way to classify certain experiences on the AAPI, so just use your judgment about how to document those hours.
- When the exact number of practicum hours or clients seen is not available, your best estimate of these hours is acceptable.
- If you are unsure about how to classify a particular aspect of your experience, consult with your DCT. In addition to being a good resource to answer this type of question, your DCT must ultimately approve of how you have documented your experience on the AAPI.

- You may include relevant work experience obtained during your graduate program as part of your practicum hours only if your program considers this experience "program sanctioned."
- You may also contact APPIC if you have any questions about completing the AAPI. Contact information is provided in the AAPI instructions.

GOALS AND ESSAYS

Question 9. How personal do I get in the autobiographical essay?

This question is difficult to answer because every person has a different definition of "personal" information. Some essay readers may like to see some details about a prospective intern's personal (e.g., childhood) experiences, but others may find this information irrelevant. Maybe the best answer here is embedded in the preponderance of the comments that internship faculty make about this essay. That is, when internship faculty comment on pitfalls in autobiographical essays, they usually focus on those that are "too personal" rather than those that were not revealing enough. "Too personal" usually relates to discussion of numerous difficult life experiences that have shaped a student's life or to the disclosure of a great deal of personal information that does not necessarily relate to a prospective intern's professional development. On the other hand, some sites argue that students' essays are often not personal enough. Given this anecdotal information, it may be wise to present a balanced view of your personal experiences and to link those experiences directly to your professional development.

Question 10. I am sacrificing some of my goals so that I can complete internship in my immediate geographic region. How do I write my essays to communicate "fit" and be authentic at the same time?

This question suggests that personal values and goals are interfacing with professional values and goals. We believe that striving for that kind of balance is a good approach to the application and selection process. Achieving that balance may be difficult in a selection system that is characterized by "matching" training goals with opportunities. Our belief, however, is that most internship sites offer diverse, quality training experiences that will benefit students and promote their development. Thus, we contend that each internship has something good to offer, and just because it is close to home, its quality should not be discounted. By identifying your goals and values and objectively linking those to the opportunities afforded, you may realize that the "site next door" actually is a good fit and will promote your development. Hence, you can remain local and be "authentic" about fit.

SUPPLEMENTARY MATERIALS

Question 11. 1 have seen curricula vitae (CVs) that include personal information such as age, marital status, number of children, citizenship, place of birth, and so forth. Any insights about whether selection committees expect or want this information on applicants' CVs would be appreciated.

Our recommendation is to not include such information. Having that information on a CV is definitely not an expectation of selection committees, and the vast majority of applicants do not include it.

Question 12. How many letters of recommendation are considered enough but not excessive? Can references be sent to me and I, in turn, forward them to the sites I'm applying to?

There is no clear agreement about this. Many people think you should send only the number of letters requested, whereas others believe that sending one additional letter is a good idea. Under no circumstances should you send more than one additional letter, because this is more likely to annoy selection committees than be helpful to your application.

The advantages of sending an extra letter are that you are protected if one gets lost (or if one of your recommenders does not meet the deadline) and it can provide an extra perspective on your competence, which can be helpful to the site. On the other hand, selection committees have a lot of material to read already; in fact, some sites will not read an additional letter if it is included. In addition, having an extra letter requires one other person to take the time to write a letter for you.

Remember that when it comes to letters of recommendation, more is not necessarily better. For example, having three stellar letters is far better than submitting three stellar letters plus one good or average letter. So, the bottom line is that there is no right answer to this question. Consider sending either just the number of letters requested or, at most, one more.

Different sites have different requirements about how they want the recommendation letters to arrive (either accompanying the AAPI or directly from each person who is writing a letter). If a site does not specify a method, then it is up to you to decide.

Question 13. Once I have submitted my applications, when can I expect to hear back from sites?

The APPIC Match policies require sites to list their interview notification dates (the dates by which these programs are required to notify applicants as to whether or not they received an interview) in the *APPIC Directory Online.* Although APPIC recommends that sites adopt a December 15 interview notification date, sites are in fact free to set their own timelines. APPIC instituted this policy several years ago to make it easier for applicants to construct their travel itineraries.

If you have not heard from a site by the end of the day on its designated interview notification date, you may wish to contact the site (e.g., via phone or e-mail) the next day or soon thereafter to inquire about your status. In this situation, you may also wish to use APPIC's Informal Problem Consultation and Resolution service to confidentially let APPIC know that a site didn't meet its obligation to notify applicants by its published interview notification date.

THE INTERVIEW

Question 14. Group interviews seem to bring out my competitive spirit. How do I go about "competing" without appearing overly competitive and defensive?

Interviews provide internship faculty with considerable information about applicants' interpersonal skills and coping resources. "Competitiveness" typically is not what faculty are looking for because they may infer that this competitive spirit will cause problems with other interns over the course of a training year. Therefore, we encourage you to approach these interview situations with "getting along" rather than "winning the slot" as your number one goal; if you get along with people, you have a better chance of winning the slot. Remember also that the individuals that you interview alongside will be your future colleagues throughout your professional life. It may be in your best interest to learn from, interact well with, and make a good impression on your colleagues, as well.

Question 15. Will I have to interpret a Rorschach on my interviews?

We do not have hard data on this issue, but anecdotal information suggests that very few sites and internship faculty require students to demonstrate specific skills during interviews. That is, rarely will you be handed a Rorschach protocol or an SPSS printout and be asked to "interpret this." However, you may be asked to present an example of a client with whom you have worked or conceptualize cases on the basis of a handful of "facts," or you may be presented a clinical scenario that requires you to comment on how you would use your multicultural competence to address client needs. Be sure to practice a brief case presentation before you leave for your interviews.

Question 16. What can I expect to happen after the interview? Will sites stay in contact with me?

Again, contact varies significantly depending on the internship program. Some sites will have no further contact with you after the interview process is over, whereas others may contact you if they have additional questions or to give you an opportunity to ask questions of them. You really should not try to infer much about a site's interest in you based on how much postinterview contact they do or do not initiate—it really depends on their own approach to the process.

And, as emphasized in Chapter 6, "The Match," any inferences that you may make about sites' interest in you should not in any way affect how you rank those sites. Remember that your rankings for the Match should be based only on your true preferences and should not be influenced by what you perceive as the likelihood that you will be matched to any site.

Question 17. What if I have questions for a site—maybe about their program, or whether they have received my application? Is it OK to contact them? If so, what is the best way to do so?

Many students hesitate to contact sites to ask questions about the program, application procedures, timelines, and so on, for fear of bothering the training director and negatively affecting their application. However, we encourage you to contact a site directly whenever you have questions. The *APPIC Directory* lists the ways in which a site prefers to be contacted (e.g., telephone, e-mail). Most training directors are eager to have you know as much about their program as possible—remember, they are trying to put their best face forward also. One caveat: Review the program's website and/or brochure, as well as their *APPIC Directory Online* information, before contacting a site, as it is best not to ask questions that are already answered in their materials.

In addition, one of the best ways to find out about a site is to talk with the current interns directly. Interns are often more likely to give you a balanced perspective about the internship experience at the site, including strengths and weaknesses of the program. Training directors understand that applicants like to talk with their current interns and will be happy to arrange for you to talk with one of them.

You also should remember that every contact that you have with a site could potentially be a part of the interview process. Even your interactions with support staff—positive or negative—might find their way to the selection committee. Sometimes current interns are members of the selection committee, and thus your contacts with them might ultimately be a part of the interview process as well.

Question 18. What should I do if someone at an internship site violates the Match policies by asking me about how I intend to rank that site?

We hope that this will not happen to you, as most training directors are very careful and do not want to put internship applicants in such an uncomfortable position (nor do they want to get into trouble with APPIC!). But if this does happen, the best approach is to politely remind the interviewer that the APPIC Match policies do not permit you to share such information with him or her. Of course, this can result in a brief uncomfortable moment in the interview and possibly some embarrassment on the part of the interviewer, but it can provide an important reminder to the interviewer about the policies. And, in most instances, the interviewer will gain respect for you for having the courage to appropriately set this boundary during an interview.

Most of the time, such policy violations are the result of mistakes, misunderstandings, or miscommunications among the training staff, and rarely are intentional or malicious acts.

You should also remember that APPIC has both an informal problem resolution process and a formal complaint process that can be used to address violations of the Match policies. Thus, you should not hesitate to contact APPIC if you need assistance in resolving a difficult situation.

Question 19. What should I do if someone at an internship site asks me a question on an interview that is illegal?

According to an APPIC newsletter article by Mona Koppel Mitnick, Esq., an attorney and the public member of the APPIC Board of Directors, the following questions should not be asked of internship applicants unless they relate to actual qualifications for the position or the applicant raises the issue himself or herself: marital or family status, religion, physical condition or limitations, sexual preference, or physical or mental health status. This is not an exhaustive list, and there may be certain conditions in which some of these questions may be legally asked.

If you are asked such a question during an interview, there are a couple of ways to respond. One approach is to let the interviewer know that you are not comfortable answering the question or that you believe that it is not an appropriate question for an interview. However, we do recognize that some applicants may be hesitant to respond this way out of concern that it will lead to a negative response by the interviewer or that they will be seen as resistant or uncooperative.

Another approach is to simply answer the question in the moment but to take some form of action at a later time. For example, you could later (either after the interview or after the entire selection process) contact the training director to inform him or her that you were asked a question that you believe may be illegal. Our belief is that most training directors will be grateful that you have brought this issue to their attention so that they can take corrective action with the individual involved.

Alternatively, you can use APPIC's informal problem resolution or formal complaint processes to address the situation. In particular, if you are unsure about the legality or appropriateness of a particular interview question, the informal problem resolution process can provide an opportunity for you to discuss the situation confidentially with an APPIC representative and review the options that might be available to you.

Also, keep in mind that there are some interview questions that you may consider to be inappropriate but that are legal nonetheless. A good example is, "Tell us about the other sites to which you have applied for an internship." Some applicants find this question to be somewhat intrusive and unnecessary, but there is nothing that prevents a site from asking it.

Additional resources on the topic of legal and illegal interview questions may be found at the APPIC website (http://www.appic.org).

THE MATCH

Question 20. When should I register for the Match? What happens if I register late and do not get my applicant code number in time to provide it to sites on the AAPI?

Although APPIC recommends that all applicants register by December 1, we generally recommend that you register for the Match in September or early October to receive your applicant code number and include it on the AAPI. However, if you are unsure about whether or not you will be applying for internship in the coming year, you may wish to wait until closer to the deadline, as the Match registration fee is nonrefundable and nontransferable to a future year. If you register later in the process, don't worry—simply enter it into the AAPI Online once you do receive it.

Question 21. Both my partner and I will be applying for psychology internships this year. Are there any special procedures that are available for us?

Any two applicants who wish to coordinate their choices of internship may participate in the Match as a "couple." Most couples will find it advantageous to use these special procedures to attempt to secure internships in the same geographic area. More information is available on the APPIC and NMS websites.

Question 22. What considerations do I use when constructing my rankings?

The most important thing to remember is to simply rank internship programs in the order in which you want them. That is all you need to worry about. Do not, under any circumstances, take into account such things as how you believe a site is ranking you, how well you think you have impressed a site, the feedback that you are getting from a site, and so forth. The matching program has been specifically designed to allow you to rank sites in the order in which you want them, without consideration of these other factors, in order to be assured of receiving the best match possible.

Question 23. What if I do not know whether I am still under consideration by a site? Should I still rank that site?

As long as you are still interested in the site, you should rank it. It does not hurt you in any way to rank a site that does not ultimately rank you. If that happens, the computer will simply skip over that site on your list and proceed with the next ranked site, without having reduced your chances of being matched to any other site on your list.

Question 24. I am hesitant to give up my top ranking to a site that does not seem all that interested in me.

This is an understandable concern, but it is not something that you need to be concerned about. If a site is truly your top choice, then you should absolutely, positively rank that site as number one on your list regardless of how interested in you they seem. By doing so, you will not have reduced your chances of being matched to other sites on your list if your top-ranked site does not work out.

Question 25. I just received a letter today from one of my ranked sites stating that I was no longer under consideration. But I have already submitted my rankings! Any suggestions?

Not to worry: The computer will simply skip over that program on your list—it will not affect your chances of getting matched to any of your other sites. In other words, even if you did log in to the Rank Order List Input and Confirmation system to remove that program from your list, it would not matter—you would still be matched to the exact same program as if you had left it on your list.

Question 26. Given my current circumstances, I am not completely sure that I want to attend internship during the coming year. Should I still submit a rank order list (ROL)?

You should submit an ROL only if you are absolutely, positively, 100% sure that you are ready to accept the internship to which you are matched. The APPIC Match is binding, and you are not permitted to change your mind once matched to an internship site. Thus, if you are unsure about your ability to commit to internship during the coming year, then you should not submit an ROL.

Question 27. What if I decide that I do not like the internship site to which I have been matched? Is it possible to change my mind?

No, you are required to attend the internship program to which you are matched. Thus, if a program is not an acceptable option for you, you should not include it on your ROL.

Question 28. What is the first thing that I should do if I am not matched to an internship site in Phase I of the Match?

First, remember that you still have an opportunity to apply for internship positions in Phase II of the Match and the Post-Match Vacancy Service. Second, talk with people. Talking with your significant others will give you the support you need and some guidance about how to proceed. Talking with your academic advisor and your DCT will help you identify the necessary steps to search for available internship slots that are acceptable to you and to important others in your life. Be sure to review the material in this workbook (Chapter 6) that discusses Phase II and the APPIC Post-Match Vacancy Service, along with the extensive instructions and suggestions for applicants located on the APPIC website.

Question 29. I think that a site may have violated an APPIC policy. I am uncertain if their behavior was really a violation, and even if it was, whether I should risk reporting it. What should I do?

Probably the best approach is to discuss the situation with APPIC's Informal Problem Consultation representative (see http://www.appic.org and click on "Problem Consultation" for contact information for this person). Your initial contact with this consultant will be to confidentially discuss the situation and is an opportunity for you to better understand your options for resolution of the problem. Contacting APPIC does not obligate you to take any action or to file a complaint.

The Match policies were put into place to make the internship application and Match process one that is fair and respectful for students and sites alike. Although violations are uncommon, they do occur. Students often wonder whether reporting a potential violation will have negative consequences for them or their chances of securing an internship. This is rarely the case. Your situation can be handled informally or formally, depending on the nature of your complaint. If the problem is serious, it is important for you to inform APPIC of the problem because one of their member sites may not be complying with the rules it agreed to abide by.

Question 30. I am a Canadian student seeking a United States internship [or a United States student seeking a Canadian internship]. What should I be aware of or concerned about?

International students must primarily be concerned about obtaining the appropriate visa status to have an educational/training experience in the host country. Internship is not considered a job, even though a stipend is earned, but often special visa status must be requested and granted. For more information, consult *Studying Psychology in the United States: Expert Guidance for International Students* (APA, 2008; see the Appendix) for a discussion about internship, postdoc, and licensure issues for international students. Also consider consulting with the Canadian Psychological Association and visiting the APPIC website for more information.

Question 31. I have more questions that have not been addressed in this chapter. What do I do?

You have several options available. First, ask your DCT or other faculty members for assistance. Second, you may post your questions to the APPIC INTERN-NETWORK e-mail list (see the Appendix). This list is moderated by Dr. Greg Keilin, the APPIC Match coordinator, and also has a number of training directors and previous years' applicants who monitor the list and can help answer your questions. You can also contact Dr. Keilin directly via e-mail (gkeilin@mail.utexas.edu) or telephone (512-475-6949) and he will be happy to assist you.

8 ADVICE FOR DCTs OF STUDENTS IN THE INTERNSHIP APPLICATION PROCESS

As a director of clinical training (DCT), you already are aware that the students in your program applying for internship likely are experiencing a significant amount of anxiety related to the application process. To some extent, this anxiety is normative and adaptive. As the imbalance between available slots and applicants increases, the potential for being "unmatched" is very real. However, data still indicate that over three quarters of students do match, and almost half of all students who match receive an offer from their first-choice site. These statistics have been relatively consistent for many years, and your students previously have been quite successful when participating in very competitive application processes (i.e., applying to doctoral programs in professional psychology).

Your job as DCT, in large part, is to help your students manage their anxiety as much as possible. However, there are also several specific ways in which you may be able to help your students prepare a strong application and be optimally prepared for the rigorous application process. This chapter outlines a series of specific strategies that may be useful for you when advising students in your program. The application process also has changed significantly over the past several years. Several of these changes also are discussed below.

STEP 1. ORIENTING STUDENTS TO THE APPLICATION PROCESS

Most application deadlines are at the end of October through late November in the academic year of the Match. Several months earlier, your students likely will begin to peruse the online directory of internship programs at http://www.appic.org. The summer is often a good time for a general meeting with your students. During this meeting, you may want to inform them of several points listed below.

- A good first step for the applicant in this process is to determine his or her training goals for the internship year and beyond. These goals can help guide an

DOI: 10.1037/13946-008
Internships in Psychology: The APAGS Workbook for Writing Successful Applications and Finding the Right Fit, Third Edition, by C. Williams-Nickelson, M. J. Prinstein, and W. G. Keilin

applicant through each stage of the process (i.e., selecting sites, writing essays, answering interview questions, and ranking sites) and will help the applicant remain focused and grounded for the next several months. See Chapter 3 for more information on setting training goals.

- The *APPIC Directory* is updated in the spring of each year. It is important to visit the site periodically and to use both broad and narrow searches to help capture sites that may be the best fit for their training needs.
- It is important to immediately subscribe to APPIC's MATCH-NEWS LISTSERV for important updates throughout the process. The INTERN-NETWORK e-mail discussion list may also be of interest to some, but it often increases anxiety for many who eavesdrop on very detailed conversations and questions among other applicants.
- You may wish to share a list of sites that are common among students in your program. Students tend to be most successful when applying to sites that are familiar with your doctoral program and have previously selected your students as successful interns.
- Remind students that they will need to complete the application process at the same time as other program requirements. Many students report that the internship process takes as much time and energy as would one moderately intensive graduate course during the fall semester, students are mostly unavailable (physically or psychologically) for the month of January, and many students find their productivity waning between February and June. It is best to plan for these time commitments early.
- Many students appreciate a timeline with suggested deadlines (see Exhibit 8.1).

A Reframe

In addition to a review of these application-related tasks, your first meeting with students also may include a reframe on the internship application process. Many of your students will enter this process with a single goal: to match. But the process they are about to undertake actually offers much more.

Exhibit 8.1. *Internship Application Timeline*

Deadline	Task
September 1	Construct (almost) final list of sites to which you are applying (15 max).
September 20	Compute clinical hours.
	Update CV.
	Order transcripts.
	Select and notify faculty who will write you letters of recommendation.
	Register for the MATCH.
	Make list of supplemental materials or special requirements needed for each application.
October 10	Complete first draft of essays.
October 20	Complete final draft of essays.
	Make sure all letters of recommendation have been submitted to the online application portal.
October 25	Begin process of uploading and routing all application materials online.

The internship application process is an outstanding professional development opportunity. Rarely do our students get a chance to reflect on their experiences, review their career goals, and think about how they are a unique, autonomous, and efficacious psychologist. Many students also have a narrow vision of the workplace for psychologists, simply because they have had substantial exposure to only one model of psychological research and practice (i.e., in your program). This process, if taken seriously, will change that. The essays are self-reflective exercises. If they do the essays well, students learn a great deal about themselves while writing (and rewriting) them. The interviews are a "world tour" of the field, the many settings and roles of psychologists within it, and an opportunity for social networking that will likely be relevant to their professional experiences well beyond the internship year. The internship application process is another educational experience in the progression of experiences that students get in doctoral training. Like all other educational experiences in your program, this one can be overseen by you and your faculty in a way that helps students get the most out of it.

To facilitate your students' professional development, use your meeting at the start of the process to ask your students questions, such as these:

- Where would you like to be professionally in 5 to 10 years? What specific skills/ experiences do you need to get from where you are today to where you want to be?
- Imagine that another student in this program had the exact same research, practica, and didactic experiences as you "on paper." What makes you different from that other student? Think beyond what training you had and contemplate your reactions, impressions, observations, and reflections to each training experience.
- What do you think is important in the field? What contribution do you want to make?
- How do your beliefs about your research area differ from those of your research advisor? How do your ideas about clinical work differ from those of your clinical supervisor?

Once students have truly contemplated these types of questions, you will notice a substantial improvement in the quality of their essays and in their responses to mock interview questions. Challenging them to continually think of these issues at the start of the application process also will help them gain an educational experience that will endure, whether or not they match.

STEP 2: HELPING STUDENTS COMPLETE THEIR APPLICATIONS Although many of your students will be able to complete most parts of the application autonomously, it is not a bad idea to take a quick look at each part of their application. In particular, many students have little experience with preparing a formal curriculum vitae (CV) before this stage in their career. Carefully reviewing and proofreading their CV can be extremely helpful for them. It may be useful to circulate the CVs of prior students who applied to internship to help folks understand how prior graduate experiences from your program traditionally are documented on a CV.

Similarly, many students have questions about how to calculate their hours. You should familiarize yourself with the general instructions for calculating hours by reviewing suggestions at http://www.appic.org and by reviewing the instructions in the AAPI Online itself (note that it is perfectly acceptable for you to create a free AAPI

Online account so you can see its functionality firsthand). If you are unable to answer a question from a student about how certain hours are to be counted, you may contact the AAPI Online Coordinator (see the "Contact" page on the APPIC website for contact information).

A quick review of students' list of sites also can be enormously helpful. It is critical that students know not to apply to a limited geographic area, if at all possible, because this is one of the strongest predictors of being unmatched. It also is important to make sure that students apply to a reasonable number of places (between 10 and 15) and to remind them that at least a few of them should be sites where your program has placed interns before.

It is a good idea to review each student's list of referees. Although little empirical data are available regarding the factors in a letter of recommendation that are associated with positive internship outcomes (particularly since the vast majority of recommendation letters are uniformly glowing), some evidence suggests that letters *predominantly* from outside the formal graduate program or from referees who do not have doctoral training in psychology, or, conversely, letters missing from one's primary mentor can raise concerns among internship selection committees.

Essays

Once students reach the internship application process, most of the content in their application is no longer malleable. Their clinical hours and CV-related experiences already are accrued. Their referees' professional impressions largely have been formed. Their transcripts can no longer be improved meaningfully. However, students still can substantially influence their outcome by working conscientiously and thoughtfully on their essays, and as DCT, you can be a tremendous help to them in this process.

In this workbook, we have offered substantial suggestions, guidelines, and directions for successfully completing the essays that are part of the internship application process. In addition to reviewing these suggestions, there are several specific ways in which you can help students create effective essays.

1. Do students' essays help distinguish them as a unique psychologist? It is quite common for students to write essays with a broad statement of experiences and interests. Often, students have not challenged themselves to think of their expertise as valid, unique, and distinct. Your encouragement and feedback, from the perspective of a training director who can identify unique strengths of each student's training, can help students to communicate a clear identity in their essays that will help them seem unique and interesting to the selection committee.

2. Do students describe their accomplishments too modestly in their essays? Our professional culture does not involve self-promotional skills, at least as much as is seen in some other professions. In fact, psychology trainees often are plagued by "impostor syndrome" and uncertainty regarding their own skills. The internship application process requires some sales ability, however. You may be surprised how often students neglect to include prestigious honors in their autobiographical statement! As one who reads many applications (for graduate school admissions), you are very aware that such important selling points often

need to be repeated in more than one place in one's materials to catch the attention of a bleary-eyed reviewer.

3. Are students' training goals realistic? Many students have accrued substantial exposure to a university-based clinical service system during graduate school but have not yet learned what other types of clinical experiences may be available at an internship setting. By reviewing their goals and helping students express them clearly, and repeatedly, throughout their essays, you will help your students to communicate a match to each training program.

4. Does the autobiographical statement seem too familiar? Commonly, a student's autobiographical statement reads like the story of why he or she chose graduate school in professional psychology—perhaps similar in tone and content to what you read years ago when this student first applied to your program. It is far more important for this essay to tell the story that started with graduate school admission, ending with the rationale for specific internship training goals. Because all students applying for internship have somehow found their way to the profession of psychology and successfully gained entry into a doctoral program, that part of the story is typically not relevant or helpful in establishing a distinct identity as a psychologist. An autobiographical statement that helps the internship committee identify unique graduate-level skills, accomplishments, and interests is more useful at this stage. Also, keep in mind that some sites may want students to include autobiographical details that are not necessarily professionally relevant. Advise students on the level of personal detail that feels appropriate and offer feedback to students that helps them develop an essay that is uniquely theirs (i.e., that clearly conveys their personality and interests).

5. Do essays read like term papers? The second and third essays in the internship application process ask about case conceptualization/orientation, and multiculturalism/diversity, respectively. Students' responses to these questions often read like a final exam from a graduate course. While this may communicate a strong knowledge base, such a style does not help to differentiate the applicant from others who have had graduate training. Help your students express their opinions and unique viewpoints in response to these questions. A potential supervisor likely will be most enthusiastic about an applicant who will be stimulating in supervision. These essays can be used to help communicate such a quality.

6. Last, are the "fit" arguments in the cover letter and essays compelling? From your experience reading hundreds of applications, you already know what works in an essay. As with graduate student applicants, intern applicants also need to communicate enthusiasm and a well-thought-out rationale for wanting X training at Y site.

STEP 3: PREPARING STUDENTS FOR INTERVIEWS

Interviews are happening earlier and earlier each year; some are scheduled for the first week in December. It is best to meet with intern applicants and prepare them for "interview season" as early as possible.

First, it is probably very important to inform students that applicants will hear from internship sites at very different times over the months of November and December. Even interview invitations from the same site can reach your students weeks apart. It will be important for them to resist the temptation to compare themselves to others. Fellow applicants' news has no bearing on the news they may soon receive.

The process of scheduling intern applicants into available interview dates has turned lately into a subtle form of guerilla warfare. Program assistants seem to call applicants earlier and earlier, sometimes asking for schedule commitments on the spot, and without much patience, grace, or understanding of the complexities from the applicants' perspective. To be sure, scheduling is complex and hectic on both ends of the process, and the competition on all sides has become more intense. As a result, students often become quite rattled and hesitant when attempting to negotiate the complexities of scheduling. You can be an excellent sounding board for these students by offering feedback on whether their concerns and requests are appropriate, professional, and communicated adequately.

As DCT, you surely will want to discuss the protocol you wish your students to follow should they have to reschedule, cancel, or decline an interview. The behavior of this year's applicants may affect the success of next year's applicants to a given site. From a program perspective, you may wish to offer clear guidance on how you want applicants to handle such situations.

Although this can be quite difficult, this also is a good time to sit down with an applicant from your program who you suspect may not navigate the interview process successfully. Internship sites increasingly look toward doctoral programs and their DCTs as the gatekeepers for the profession. If you do have a student whose social skills, attire, or professional presentation contributes to a suboptimal first impression, it is very useful to counsel that student accordingly before he or she moves on to the interview stage of this process.

Many doctoral programs provide substantial support during the application process but considerably less for the internship interviews—usually because they assume that students who receive interviews will ultimately be successful in securing a position. However, it is not at all uncommon for a highly qualified student to get many interview offers as a result of a well-written application, only to have a disappointing Match result due to poor interviewing skills. As DCT, it is imperative to remember that the competencies that make a student a wonderful researcher, teacher, or clinician are very different from the competencies required to be an effective interviewee. Thus, even your best students may need substantial assistance with the interview process.

Regardless of their past success in your program, then, all students can benefit from a brief role play with you before their first interview. The interview role play offers an excellent (a) exposure exercise to reduce anxiety; (b) confidence-building exercise, as students typically realize that interviewing is something they already know how to do well; (c) rehearsal for answers to commonly asked questions; and (d) opportunity for feedback, including students' self-evaluation, along with your evaluation of their interview behavior.

A role play can last only 15 minutes, yet still be very effective. It may be useful to simulate both an interviewer who asks many questions and an interviewer who offers only to answer the applicants' questions. In the former scenario, it is surprising for students to realize that their answers to even the most basic questions (e.g., "What is your dissertation about?") come across as rambled or disorganized until they have had some out-loud practice. In the latter scenario, it is quite effective for students to experience the difficulty of "leading" an interview with an endless supply of questions. In a role play, many run out of questions in only 5 or 10 minutes; this is an impressive realization for students. The role play can help them appreciate how important it is for them to prepare many, many questions in advance.

It may be useful to reframe the interview experience for students. Tell them to imagine that, within an hour of the conclusion of their interview, they will have to decide whether to attend the site or not. This hypothetical exercise often helps applicants realize exactly what questions they really need to ask, and it helps them reorient the experience from a scary, unknown experience to one in which they can feel more active and authoritative.

Students universally benefit from the role play and tend to extract quite meaningful self-evaluative lessons from the experience. And it really will not take too much of your time!

Of course, in addition to students' self-impressions, students can receive invaluable feedback from you following an interview role play. Some students are unaware of their verbal and nonverbal communication style. Commonly, students do not realize that they may be too quiet to convey enthusiasm. Some are overly energetic/anxious in a manner that could make an interviewer uncomfortable. Others might think they are answering questions effectively but instead are providing overly generic or nonspecific answers, or are not answering the questions being asked. Because students typically have not practiced their interviewing skills (as an applicant) for several years before this process, it is quite common that some will experience more difficulties than you may have predicted.

Your feedback during these role plays will be most valuable if you put yourself in the role of an interviewer who is outside of academia and who does not know the student. In other words, as much as possible, be aware of your own favorable biases toward your students and the settings in which your students will interview, as this can help you listen carefully to their responses and give them the most constructive feedback.

Several programs have employed creative strategies to assist their students in preparing for an interview. For instance, some engage their career counseling services center to set up mock interviews and provide feedback to intern applicants. Notably, some of these centers will offer videotaped feedback of the mock interview. Other programs have scheduled future intern applicants to serve as interviewers for graduate school admissions the year before they apply. Adopting the perspective of an interviewer can assist enormously in preparing to attend interviews as an applicant.

STEP 4: DEBRIEFING AND RANK ORDER LISTS

Once upon a time, intern applicants could sit by their phones for hours, or days, and receive offers from various internship sites. Now, with a computer-administered matching system, the final few weeks of the internship application process have changed considerably. In fact, Match Day is now a specific day, and applicants engage in an extraordinary set of cognitive processes once interviews have concluded.

A meeting with all internship applicants when the "interview season" is over can be quite helpful for your program. First, your students will appreciate the opportunity for emotional processing following their trials and tribulations out in the internship world. Receiving peer support for their more troubling or confusing experiences, laughing together about their unexpected hurdles, and commiserating as a group over the long wait to come can be a nice way to debrief once your students come home. Many of your students may already have friendships that would allow for this type of interaction without the need for you to formally organize it. However, within a single internship "class" there may be a single student who is less likely than others to have this opportunity, and your formal meeting for debriefing may give that individual a chance that he or she would not otherwise have.

Note: As DCT, it also is your job to be on the lookout for any inappropriate behavior (e.g., violation of MATCH rules and policies) that your students may have encountered while on interviews. More information is available at http://www.appic.org on grievance hotlines and resources available in such a situation.

It is critical that at this stage of the process you remind students to construct a rank order list (ROL) that reflects their true preferences regarding each site. Students should not attempt to "game" the system, and they should not be swayed inappropriately by their perceived chances of getting accepted to any given site. The computer match algorithm will not penalize a student for lowly ranking a site that is most enthusiastic about that student. In other words, a student has nothing to lose by top-ranking a "long shot"; it will not reduce his or her chances at other sites ranked lower.

It also is critical to remind students that if they rank a site, and match to that site, they are required to attend. It can be useful to ask students to imagine that they have matched to their last-ranked site and consider whether they would prefer this outcome over waiting an additional year before internship.

Applicants typically find their emotions, anxieties, and hopes to be quite confusing at this stage of the process. Some wonder how much prestige weighs in their decision. Some are confused by interactions that they have had (or not had) since their interview. Some lose sight of their internship goals at this stage of the process and need reminding to ensure that they are making decisions that make sense both professionally and personally. A brief meeting with each applicant to review their ROLs can be extremely helpful.

And then they wait. It takes a few weeks for the Match results to be completed. This is a great time to remind students of the many benefits to completing one's dissertation before they leave for internship! Working on a dissertation is an excellent distraction from the waiting game.

Students will receive their Match results on Match Day in the morning by e-mail, or on the National Matching Services website. For those students who did not secure a position, there are several ways you can be very helpful with Phase II of the Match process.

STEP 5: HELPING WITH PHASE II OF THE MATCH, IF NEEDED

Students can truly be devastated if they do not match in the internship application process. As perfectionistic and high-achieving students, they may be experiencing one of the first negative experiences of their academic lives, and they may be poorly equipped to cope with such an outcome. Students may feel hopeless, embarrassed, ashamed, confused, and quite angry, and DCTs should approach their work with a student who has not matched much as one might approach a client who recently has experienced a death in the family. Behaviors may be unpredictable, and emotions should be monitored closely.

Moreover, students who have not matched often experience uncomfortable conversations with family in the days that follow, as well as potential alienation from their graduate school peers, who may not know how to help. Meanwhile, other students from your program are quietly celebrating their successful outcome, and the unmatched student becomes further marginalized in what was previously their home.

You should be available to your students on Match Day, if possible, and attempt to mobilize the other faculty in your program to reach out with reassurance and support to anyone who does not match. An outpouring of support from faculty can be an extremely powerful way to help a student who has experienced this unexpected and disappointing outcome.

It is also advisable to help an unmatched student move from emotion-focused coping to problem-focused coping over the course of the next few days. Students must decide rather quickly whether they wish to enter the second Match. If so, there is work to be done!

Once students have received the bad news, they will need to be prepared for a very fast-moving, competitive, and hectic application process. It is best to prepare several things right away:

1. Ask your unmatched students to strongly consider their parameters for a possible internship opportunity. Are there parts of the country they would not or cannot move to? Are there internship experiences they are not willing to consider or would be unqualified to apply for?

2. Have your students redraft their cover letters, or multiple forms of their cover letters, that briefly describe their experiences and interests. Given the variety of sites any particular student may apply to in the second Match process, it is important to find time to write several different cover letter versions in just the next few days.

3. Review your students' schedules and discuss the feasibility of Phase II. In a rapid period of time, students will be asked to submit applications, participate in interviews, and rank order sites all over again. This is time consuming and psychologically draining. Help them mobilize social and instrumental support systems.

   Phase II is new, as is the Post Match Vacancy Service that follows Phase II. It is best for you to be as knowledgeable about the process as your student needs to be. Please see Chapter 6 for a detailed description of Phase II of the APPIC Match.

CONCLUSION   Students can use your support and expertise as their DCT throughout the internship application process. Although many of the suggestions listed here will take some time to follow, your students will be very grateful that you did. The internship process is stressful and hectic for them, and it is easy for them to simply be focused on finding a slot in which to complete their training. However, with your help, this process can offer a terrific opportunity for your student to grow and gain confidence as a psychologist and to match to an internship site that will cap off your training investment in each student from your program.

Appendix:
Additional Resources

Internship Workshops and Programs

The American Psychological Association of Graduate Students (APAGS) offers many resources to assist students with internship-related issues. In addition to the annual APAGS preconvention workshop, APAGS routinely offers other convention programming addressing different aspects of the internship process. For information about registration for these programs, visit the APAGS website (http://www.apa.org/apags). There are also opportunities for universities and programs to host an APAGS internship workshop on their campus, presented by the APAGS Central Office staff and often by members of the APAGS Committee. For more information about this opportunity, contact the APAGS Central Office, (202) 336-6014.

APAGS Liaison to APPIC

APAGS works closely with APPIC by sending an APAGS member liaison to all APPIC meetings. The APAGS website and the APAGS magazine, *gradPSYCH*, feature articles on the topic of internship.

APAGS Internship LISTSERV

APAGS sponsors a LISTSERV for APAGS members who are preparing for and experiencing the internship application process. The list also serves as a forum for individuals currently on internship to discuss transition and career issues. All LISTSERV subscribers may post questions to the list and contribute to the LISTSERV discussion. APAGS members may subscribe to this list by sending the following message, with a blank subject line and your signature line disabled, to

> LISTSERV@lists.apa.org
> Subscribe APAGSINTERNSHIP First-Name Last-Name
> Example: Subscribe APAGSINTERNSHIP Terry Gradley

A Survival Guide for Ethnic Minority Graduate Students

APAGS members may obtain this publication by contacting APAGS directly or from the APAGS website's members-only page. This comprehensive guide is applicable for all students in content and includes sections on mentoring, networking, stress management and balance, impostor syndrome, racism, research, teaching, obtaining funding, comprehensive exams, dissertation management, internship, and professional development.

APAGS Website

Visit the APAGS website (http://www.apa.org/apags) to learn more about APAGS and the support and resources APAGS provides to its graduate student members. Information about joining APAGS is also available on the APAGS website.

The Association of Psychology Postdoctoral and Internship Centers (APPIC) has extensive information about the Match and Post-Match Vacancy Service, APPIC e-mail lists, informal and formal problem resolution, the AAPI, and many other important documents on its website (http://www.appic.org). Students may be particularly interested in the following resources.

The MATCH-NEWS e-mail list. This free e-mail list provides up-to-date news and information about the APPIC Match. It is strongly recommended that internship applicants subscribe to this list as early as possible in the process. Subscribing to this list means that you will receive occasional e-mail messages (usually only a few per month) containing news, tips, and suggestions about how to make the most of the APPIC Match and the selection process. Only APPIC personnel are authorized to post messages to this list. To subscribe, send a blank e-mail message to subscribe-match-news@lyris.appic.org.

The INTERN-NETWORK e-mail list. This free e-mail list is intended for discussion of professional psychology internship issues among internship applicants and current interns. Many applicants use the INTERN-NETWORK list to ask questions or discuss issues related to the internship selection process. Some training directors and previous Match participants are subscribed to the list in order to assist the current year's applicants. This is an all-to-all discussion list, and any list subscriber may post messages to the list. To subscribe, send a blank e-mail message to subscribe-intern-network@lyris.appic.org.

The APPIC Directory Online. The *APPIC Directory Online* is provided as a service to students, graduate faculty, and training directors in identifying APPIC-member internship and postdoctoral training programs that are likely to meet specific training needs. The *APPIC Directory Online* provides a number of search options that allow users to quickly identify programs of interest. Visit http://www.appic.org to access the directory online.

The National Matching Services website. The APPIC Internship Matching Program is administered on behalf of APPIC by National Matching Services (NMS). Registration materials for the APPIC Match may be downloaded from this site. Applicants will find extensive information about the APPIC Match on the NMS website (http://www.natmatch.com/psychint/).

Publications

Brown, R. T. (1996). Training in professional psychology: Are we addressing the issues? *Professional Psychology, Research and Practice, 27,* 506–507. doi:10.1037/0735-7028.27.5.506

Constantine, M. G., & Keilin, W. G. (1996). Association of Postdoctoral and Internship Centers' guidelines and the internship selection process: A survey of applicants and academic and internship training directors. *Professional Psychology, Research and Practice, 27,* 308–314. doi:10.1037/0735-7028.27.3.308

Constantine, M. G., Keilin, W. G., Litwinowicz, J., & Romanus, T. (1997). Post-notification day perceptions of unplaced internship applicants and their academic training directors: Recommendations for improving future internship selection processes. *Professional Psychology, Research and Practice, 28*, 387–392. doi:10.1037/0735-7028.28.4.387

Hasan, N. T., Fouad, N. A., & Williams-Nickelson, C. (2008). *Studying psychology in the United States: Expert guidance for international students.* Washington, DC: American Psychological Association.

Holaday, M., & McPhearson, R. (1996). Standardization of the APPIC predoctoral internship application forms. *Professional Psychology, Research and Practice, 27*, 508–513. doi:10.1037/0735-7028.27.5.508

Keilin, W. G. (1998). Internship selection 30 years later: An overview of the APPIC matching program. *Professional Psychology, Research and Practice, 29*, 599–603. doi:10.1037/0735-7028.29.6.599

Keilin, W. G. (2000). Internship selection in 1999: Was the Association of Psychology Postdoctoral and Internship Centers' match a success? *Professional Psychology, Research and Practice, 31*, 281–287. doi:10.1037/0735-7028.31.3.281

Keilin, W. G., Thorn, E. E., Rodolfa, E. R., Constantine, M. G., & Kaslow, N. J. (2000). Examining the balance of internship supply and demand: 1999 Association of Psychology Postdoctoral and Internship Centers' match implications. *Professional Psychology, Research and Practice, 31*, 288–294. doi:10.1037/0735-7028.31.3.288

Lopez, S. J., & Draper, P. K. (1997). Recent developments and more internship tips: A comment on Mellott, Arden, and Cho (1997). *Professional Psychology, Research and Practice, 28*, 496–498. doi:10.1037/0735-7028.28.5.496

Lopez, S. J., & Edwardson, T. (1996). Quantifying practicum experience: A comment on Hecker, Fink, Levasseur, and Parker (1995). *Professional Psychology, Research and Practice, 27*, 514–517. doi:10.1037/0735-7028.27.5.514

Lopez, S. J., Ochlert, M. E., & Moberly, R. L. (1996). Selection criteria for American Psychological Association-accredited internship programs: A survey of training directors. *Professional Psychology, Research and Practice, 27*, 518–520. doi:10.1037/0735-7028.27.5.518

Mellott, R. N., Arden, I. A., & Cho, M. E. (1997). Preparing for internship: Tips for the prospective applicant. *Professional Psychology, Research and Practice, 28*, 190–196. doi:10.1037/0735-7028.28.2.190

Mitchell, S. L. (1996). Getting a foot in the door: The written internship application. *Professional Psychology, Research and Practice, 27*, 90–92. doi:10.1037/0735-7028.27.1.90

Oehlert, M. E., Lopez, S. J., & Sumerall, S. W. (1997). Internship application: Increased costs accompany increased competitiveness. *Professional Psychology, Research and Practice, 28*, 595–596. doi:10.1037/0735-7028.28.6.595.b

Prinstein, M. J. (Ed.). (2013). *The portable mentor: Expert guide to a successful career in psychology* (2nd ed.). New York, NY: Springer.

Rodolfa, E. R. (Ed.). (2007). The internship match: Changing the paradigm to move beyond the status quo [Special issue]. *Training and Education in Professional Psychology, 1*(4).

Stewart, A. E., & Stewart, E. A. (1996a). A decision-making technique for choosing a psychology internship. *Professional Psychology, Research and Practice, 27*, 521–526. doi:10.1037/0735-7028.27.5.521

Stewart, A. E., & Stewart, E. A. (1996b). Personal and practical considerations in selecting a psychology internship. *Professional Psychology, Research and Practice, 27*, 295–303. doi:10.1037/0735-7028.27.3.295

ABOUT THE AUTHORS

Carol Williams-Nickelson, PsyD, earned her degree from Our Lady of the Lake University in San Antonio and completed her predoctoral internship at the University of Notre Dame Counseling Center. She is a counseling psychologist and former associate executive director of the American Psychological Association of Graduate Students (APAGS) at the American Psychological Association (APA) in Washington, DC, where she oversaw all operations for the organization as their chief executive. Dr. Williams-Nickelson serves as a spokesperson and advocate for graduate students to various psychology credentialing, accrediting, educational, training, and governing boards. She now serves as the executive director and chief executive officer of the American Medical Student Association (AMSA) and AMSA Foundation. Her background includes owning and presiding over a health service organization and a consulting business. Dr. Williams-Nickelson has provided services in a variety of health care and forensic settings, including hospitals, long-term care facilities, residential treatment centers, community-based organizations, private practices, and counseling centers. Her professional interests, activities, and publications are in the areas of student advocacy and development, training and supervision, legislative advocacy, leadership, professional development, women's issues, stress, and mentoring.

Mitchell J. Prinstein, PhD, completed his doctoral degree at the University of Miami and his internship and postdoctoral fellowship at the Brown University School of Medicine. He currently is Bowman and Gordon Gray Distinguished (Term) Professor and Director of Clinical Psychology at the University of North Carolina at Chapel Hill. Dr. Prinstein's developmental psychopathology research examines interpersonal models of internalizing symptoms and health risk behaviors. He has been strongly committed to professional service and professional development for many years. Dr. Prinstein was first invited to speak about the internship application process in 1995; he served as chair of the American Psychological Association of Graduate Students and as a representative to the Association of Psychology Postdoctoral and Internship Centers in 1997. He also has served as the chair of the American Psychological Association ad hoc Committee on Early Career Psychologists. Dr. Prinstein is an editor of *The Portable Mentor: Expert Guide to a Successful Career in Psychology.* He has been a presenter at the APAGS Preconvention Workshop on the Internship Application Process for the past 12 years.

W. Gregory Keilin, PhD, completed his doctoral degree in counseling psychology at Colorado State University and his predoctoral internship at The University of Texas at Austin Counseling and Mental Health Center, where he is currently the internship training director and associate director. He is the past chair of the board of directors of the Association of Psychology Postdoctoral and Internships Centers (APPIC). He led the effort to implement the computer-based internship matching program for APPIC. He currently serves as the APPIC Match coordinator and was involved in the development of the *APPIC Directory Online* and the AAPI Online services. He is continuously working to incorporate students' feedback into decisions and policies related to the application process and the computer match system.